ZOMBIE
XI

Pete Kalu is a novelist, playwright and poet and has previously won the BBC Playwrights Award, *The Voice*/Jamaica Information Service Marcus Garvey Scholarship Award and Contact/BBC Dangerous Comedy Prize. He is a PhD Creative Writing research student at Lancaster University and has recently been signed by the National Football Museum as their artist in residence.

ZOMBIE XI

PETE KALU

hoperoad : London

HopeRoad Publishing Ltd
P O Box 55544
Exhibition Road
London SW7 2DB

www.hoperoadpublishing.com
First published by HopeRoad 2016

A CPI catalogue record of this book is
available from the British Library

Supported using public funding by
ARTS COUNCIL
ENGLAND

ISBN 978-1-908446-48-0

eISBN 978-1-908446-53-4

Printed and bound by T J International Ltd, Padstow, Cornwall, UK

For Naomi

ACKNOWLEDGEMENTS

With grateful thanks to Naomi for her zombie enthusiasms, Sarbjit Kaur for inspiration and friendship, the class at 'The Old School', Saint-Colomb-de-Lauzun, for their scary lines, Heather their teacher for her problem-solving skills and occasional rally driving, Marhaba Cafe for the good times through the years.

PART 1

ZOMBIE POWER

It's a bad day. I'm a substitute again. On the bench. And this time there's a girl on the bench with us. Can it get any worse than this?

From the get-go I knew it was going to be bad. We were gathered in the poxy changing room, under the mouldy ceiling that dripped green spores and black mould and the shells of dead insects. The cracked floor-tiles were getting the usual pounding from studs being dragged across them. Players were flicking towels, kit was being swapped, shin pads tested. In the air was all the usual howling, shouting and laughter that comes when you know you're going to be playing in a football match. I was quiet, awaiting my fate.

The coach, Mr Broderick, strode in wearing his crisp white Nike tracksuit, clutching his favourite blue clipboard. He ran his fingers through his 'Caesar' haircut and I watched his eyes flit about the room because that's what he always does first – check that his first picks are in the room. His grey eyes never sought me out. He preened his hair again, then rubbed his stubbly ginger beard, hesitating. He licked the tip of his pen and his eyes went back to the clipboard. Then he looked up and, above all that buzz, called out: 'Right lads, gather round, here's the team for today!'

We came up to the flip chart where he was standing. Sometimes he has tactics drawn up on the chart. Today it was blank.

'Here we go. The team today is …'

He named the defenders. Then the midfield. Since I'm a midfielder, when my name wasn't called there, I sat down and waited for the inevitable. Sure enough, he said the words: 'And the subs today are Eddie, Leonard … and the lovely Sheba!'

What? A girl? Everybody's jaw dropped. I looked around.

The coach rapped on the steel changing-room door in a drum roll. 'Everyone got their kit on? All righty. Come in, Sheba!'

A girl pops her head – only her head – around the changing-room door. Then the rest of her. It's definitely a girl. Breasts. Huge smile. Long legs. In the team kit. She stays in the doorway, a little nervous.

'Come on, boys, give her a clap. It takes guts for her to walk into the boys' changing room!'

A few of the team clap but most of us just gawk. The coach is always bringing new players in, that's why his nickname's The Windmill – he constantly changes. But this is a new low. Somebody's got to say something. When nobody does, I decide I'll do it myself.

'We can't play with a girl.'

The Windmill laughs. 'Leonard. Always Leonard. You were born with a scowl on your face, weren't you? Go on. Tell me why.'

'Girls aren't allowed. And anyway, boys are stronger. We'll never win with girls.'

'They are allowed, thanks to the new regulations. Up to Under 15s, in fact. And Sheba's good, she'll add something.'

The coach grabs the nets bag. 'Now everybody out on the pitch and start your warm-up. Subs, take the water bottles and the bench – good lads!'

There's a giant clatter of studs and cheering from the boys who are going to be playing as they step outside.

The sky is blazing yellow. Eddie punches me on the shoulder. Horse feints a high five, then charges into my chest instead. Everybody's trying to cheer me up. I look down at my shiny old boots, the ones I stayed up all morning polishing in case I played. I pull the zipper right up on my tracksuit so it covers my chin and walk on.

Carrying the subs' bench from the changing room to the pitch is the most humiliating thing ever. Sheba tries to help out but me and Eddie don't let her. We weave the bench through the car park. Then the tarmac's stony clatter switches to the smudgy squelch of grass. The pitch is a big sea of green. The grass has been cut so one side of the pitch is light green, the other dark. It looks good. Even the burnt-out car that lived behind the far goalposts has been dragged away (there are two big gashes where it was hauled, like the claw-marks of a giant rat). A couple of parents are on the near sideline reserved for the away team. Me and Eddie take the bench over to the far side.

Our team wins the toss and chooses downhill. The game begins – for everyone but the subs, that is. So it's Eddie, me and Sheba, rubbing shoulders on the subs' bench. There's not enough room for three on it.

We're soon losing 4:0.

Sheba nudges me. 'Girls can't play football then?'

'Dead right.'

'Let's see who can throw a ball furthest then.' She's pulling me up.

'No. Keepy-uppy.'

I figure she must be good at throw-ins, else why would she suggest that? I keep the ball up five times with my feet then kick it hard at her. She kills the ball well with her knee, flips it on to her head, then down to her ankle, then knocks it up again. It's impressive but it doesn't count because she doesn't keep it up with her feet by more than two touches.

'See?' I tell her.

Eddie has a go. He manages two, like Sheba.

'I'm the best,' I declare.

The coach is waving at us to sit down. He likes us to save our legs. Impact subs, he calls it.

It's strange, me and Eddie. He's my rival for a place on the team yet I can't help liking him. He has this smile. Eddie didn't do his homework? One Eddie smile and the teacher doesn't mind. Eddie late to the canteen at lunch? A two-second Eddie megawatt grin and the shutters roll back up and the dinner ladies serve him. Sometimes I practise in front of a mirror, trying to do Eddie's smile, but my face can't stretch that far. Eddie says he likes my miserable face as it is and I shouldn't try to change it.

I watch Sheba out of the corner of my eye. I've heard rumours about her. Once I saw a girls' football training session after school while waiting for the bus and there was one girl who swerved and flowed round the orange markers like a skier, ran up the wing like Road Runner and did this crazy throw-in using a somersaulting front flip. She looked like Sheba.

14

Sheba catches me looking at her and I look away.

'I've got three dads,' I tell Eddie. 'Beat that.'

'Whatchutalkinabout?'

Eddie's shuffled between me and Sheba and is flicking his tongue at his two big front teeth where there's something lodged between them.

'I've got my official dad, like his name is on my Birth Certificate and he works on an oil rig so I never see him. Then I've got my stepdad Mustapha, though I think he split up with my mum last month ...'

I don't know if Eddie is even listening. He wriggles his nose and sucks his teeth, his eyes on the pitch. We're defending a free kick. This huge lad is about to take it. The players in our wall are shaking like a tub of slime.

'And then Thierry Henry who's my actual dad. My biological dad.'

Eddie smooths the cabbage-y thing out from between his teeth with his tongue, wipes it into his hand, looks at it, eats it, then turns to me. 'What makes you say that?' he says.

'Was that a bogey?'

'You want one?' He's going into his nose again.

'Nooo.'

'Thierry Henry?'

So he *was* listening. I pull out my pic of Thierry Henry. 'Look.'

There's a cheer from the pitch. Our goalie's fishing the ball out of the net again.

'Nah,' says Eddie, glancing at the pic then at me.

Sheba takes the pic and looks. She squishes one eye shut and moves the pic nearer to me then further away.

'My mum used to work at Man United Hospitality,' I tell her.

15

'Man U's got their own hospital?' asks Eddie.

'Catering. The VIP zone. Where they serve avocado sandwiches.'

'Wow,' says Sheba, still squinting at the pic. 'That really is Thierry Henry.'

'Right,' I tell her. 'My mum met him there and he fancied her. And, well, you know …'

'Your mum had sex with Thierry Henry?' Sheba asks, just like that. She makes me laugh, which gets her laughing. That sets off Eddie only Eddie's trying to control it and so he's silent-laughing, his upper lip wobbling away.

Sheba hands me the pic back.

'She says he gave her "a special hug" which is my mum's word for sex. Look.' I hand her the pic again. 'I look like him, don't I?'

'Apart from the nose. And the mouth. And the chin. And the eyebrows. Yeh, absolutely,' says Sheba.

She rests an arm on my shoulder either in admiration or because she feels sorry for me, I can't tell which.

'He's talking rubbish,' pronounces Eddie. 'Don't listen to him.' Eddie gets up, snatches the ball off me and starts flinging his head at it. 'Watch my headers!'

Watching Eddie attempt headers is like watching a seal trying to skateboard, but Sheba says, 'Well done, well done,' every time there's any connection between his caveman skull and the ball. Eddie's weight is weird. He doesn't eat any more than anyone else at lunchtime – and sometimes he doesn't eat at all, just sits there chatting while we all eat. Yet he's really big.

In the next field there's a dungeon-like building with girders holding it up. It's just there, for no reason. The dungeon has a hood thing on top of it that is exactly the shape of a UFO landing craft. The hood floats up and down if you really stare at it. I tell Eddie to watch and it doesn't get weirder than that, does it? But Eddie shouts back it's only a gas storage tank, duh.

I stare and stare. It's definitely moving. It starts to light up. Suddenly this blinding white flash shoots out of the UFO hood thing and strikes me. Every single cell in my body tingles. It's a feeling that's painful and beautiful at the same time. My ears ring like crazy. Drrrrr Dirrrrrr. Drrrrr Dirrrrr. My eyes have changed. They've become X-ray eyes. I can see zombies walking around. I can hear the heartbeat of every player on the pitch. The sensations fade. Everything returns to normal. I look around. Nobody's noticed. Everybody's behaving like nothing happened. I shrug it off. Maybe I should have eaten more cornflakes for breakfast.

I look up. Eddie's still heading the ball back and forward with Sheba. *Sheba.* What kind of name is that? It sounds like a cat. She makes all these noises while Eddie does his moves with the ball. *Ooh. Ah. Yes. Umm. Right. Ooh.* I almost turn round thinking maybe Lionel Messi is visiting our school, Ducie High. I know she's encouraging him and if anybody needs encouragement it's Eddie. They're laughing now. I imagine Sheba's eyes. There's a sparkle in them that's part mischief, part something else. I'm about to turn round when I get a text from my mum.

Never mind Lenny darling, don't give up hope. One day you'll be a match winner! Love you loads. xxxxMumxxxx

So many soppy kisses. Lucky Eddie and Sheba can't see.

'There's a hair's breadth between winning and losing,' Eddie's telling Sheba, like he's some Philosophy King. The

17

two of them are back on the bench. Half-time's been and gone. The score is 8:0.

Sheba nods. 'That's so true, Smiler,' she says.

She even knows his nickname now. I make a note to find a philosophy book from the library.

'If you're measuring in hairs,' I tell Eddie, 'there's a hundred wig shops of hairs between *us* winning and losing.'

Eddie laughs like I just told a great joke. Which annoys me even more. He always sees the bright side, Eddie. I notice his laugh is higher now that Sheba's with us. Is he turning into a girl himself?

'Warm up, guys!'

The Windmill has come over. Mr Broderick always waits till ten minutes before the end of the match, when we've lost anyway, before he brings any subs on. Our team's shoulders are all hunched and they've stopped chasing the ball. The other team are strutting around, putting fancy flourishes to their passes.

'Go on, Lenny,' the coach calls over. 'Warm up, lad!'

I can't be bothered. Most times he doesn't even give us five minutes' play.

Eddie's running like a hamster in a wheel. Sheba's doing this wavy-arms-touchy-toes stuff. She says it's her gymnastics routine and it makes you more flexible. Eddie copies her and falls on his backside, though he tries to style it out by going straight into a press-up.

Remember that thought I had? That it can't get any more humiliating than this? It does. The coach sends Sheba on for the last five minutes. Me and Eddie are left on the bench. We lose 9:0.

'See you on the bench next week, Eddie,' I say.

'Nah. I'll be playing next week.'

And I think, Yeh, Eddie's an optimist.

As we trudge off, I take a backwards glance. The wining team is throwing their captain up in the air. His head's so big it blocks out the sun. Behind them, the sun hits the gas storage tank. It looks as if it's fizzling at every corner.

Sheba leans her head into my back as we're walking off the pitch.

'Your time will come to shine,' she says, then rubs my shoulder. I force a smile for her. Maybe it's OK to have a girl in the team. She's about to say something else when Eddie gallops up and bounces a ball off my head. We split at the changing-room doors. She has the girls' changing room all to herself.

Our changing room isn't exactly a bundle of laughs. 'Only nine,' the coach goes. 'Sheba did a great job patching up the midfield. Andrew, nice tries with the heading. Nine is not bad.'

The changing room is the same changing room that we stepped out of two hours ago. Yet somehow it's sadder now. The floor-tiles are grottier. The pipes noisier and leakier. The smells stenchier. Horse throws his boots at a wall. Nobody's cheering and joking like before the match. We're on the longest losing run ever recorded in the league. The most number of goals let in ever.

I sigh.

'Lenny, Lenny, before you start, I don't want to hear.'

I've not said a word and I wasn't about to.

'I can't help my sighs,' I explain. 'It's an Involuntary Human Reflex.'

That gets a laugh. People cheer up a little. I change out of my kit. I don't bother showering — after all, I didn't even play, did I, so I'm spotless — and head for home. I duck into the public library on the way. It's a really old building and it's got a sign on it that says it's about to be demolished. Normally I shoot straight to football books and the Horror section. This time I turn to Philosophy. There's a book on the shelves called *Philosophy Book: Philosophy for the Philosophical*. Triple Philosophy, I think. That'll beat Eddie's single philosophy. I search pocket after pocket but I can't find my library ticket. I really need this book. I shove it in my bag.

As I'm running for the bus and away from the librarian's shouts, I hear my boots knocking together in my boots bag. They'll be as shiny as when I pulled them on. I'd love to come home one day with proper dirty boots.

I'm about to get on the bus when the driver closes the doors in my face. Everybody has days like this, I tell myself. I will enjoy walking three miles home in the freezing cold. Driver, you've made my day.

The bin lorries have just gone so our street pongs. I sling my bag on the sofa and Mum nuzzles my head. I think maybe she's checking if I've been smoking. 'Look what I've got,' she says when she's finished sniffing my hair. She picks up this ball of black fluff and holds it in her hands.

'That's wonderful, Mum.' So now we have a kitten to go with the two cats. I stroke it once then put it down. It meows and dashes under the sofa.

My sister is sitting in her corner of the room with a monster new sewing machine that has a huge spindly metal bit coming out of it like the nose of a mutant beetle.

'What's that?' I ask.

'Good afternoon, lickle brother,' she replies. 'This here is an overlocker. You have a nice day at school?'

'No,' I say. I watch her running some material through it. She's good, my sister. She makes costumes for fancy dress shops and events. She has a website and everything. When I say she's good, I mean at sewing and making things, I don't mean morally good. Her overlocker's probably stolen to order from a factory somewhere by one of her many boyfriends.

'Gary got it me at an auction,' Carla says. She's all smiles, showing off that she can read my mind.

Gary. Who has to borrow his bus fare home from our mum even though he's eighteen like Carla. The same Gary who likes to lick Carla's forehead first thing, when he calls round. Yuk. This is what I put up with.

I plonk myself on the sofa. The TV has been acting up for the last week and won't switch on. I see my favourite book under the TV and pick it up. *World Cup Winners 1966: How We Did It*. My Birth Certificate Dad left it and it has these amazing photos of football legends frozen in time. My dad loved football, Mum says. I wonder whether, if I got really brilliant at football, maybe he would come and watch me. Mum says even if he doesn't, she'll come, as soon as I'm playing, not a substitute.

I stare at the book, trying to guess which player my dad rated best. They're all wearing this ancient kit and blunt scissor haircuts, like they've just left the Army. The crowds watching them are huge. I imagine swaying in the middle of that crowd.

One of Mum's cats jumps up on the mantelpiece. It's then I notice: the photo-frame under the mirror is empty. It used to have a photo of Mustapha in it.

'What happened to Mustapha, Mum – where's his photo gone?'

Mum wanders into the living room from feeding the cats, who are all now noisily gobbling dried food. She shrugs. 'I traded him in.'

'What do you mean?' I wonder why adults always talk in riddles.

Carla's sewing machine pauses from its infernal buzzing. She wants to know too.

'I got rid of him weeks ago, didn't you notice? Then with all the money I would have spent on his birthday and sorting out his debts and that, I bought a car. Fiat Punto. Yellow. Only 146,000 miles on the clock. It's outside. Didn't you see it?'

Carla flicks at the net curtains and does a squeal. 'Mum, we've really got a new car?'

'Newish,' she says.

Carla runs and gives Mum a big kiss so she obviously wants a lift somewhere tonight. My sister's arms stay laced around Mum's neck. I join them in a hug because I can see Mum's so happy even though she's playing it cool – she's wanted a car for ages. I love my mum's giggly laugh and the smell of her. Me and my sister's arms link round Mum until she says, 'Get off! Get off!' but she's loving it. My sister's skin's light brown and she's tall. I'm dark, 'like richest cinnamon', Mum says, and short compared to Carla. Yet Mum says we've got the same dad.

'Oh I'm so happy for you, Mum,' my sister gushes, when we finally let Mum go. 'Do you need any help in the kitchen?'

That's what it takes for my sister to help Mum out. A new car. Hmmph.

The kitten moseys over to me. It's got a ridiculous face with spiky black hair, beady black and yellow eyes and granddad whiskers sprouting out of its eyelids and cheeks. Despite its looks, I let it curl up on me.

From the bottom of my boots bag, I pull out the *Philosophy Book*, fresh from the library, and flick through it. It has chapter headings including *Why You Should Question Everything, What Is the Meaning of Life, What the Ancient Egyptians Knew* and *How to Find the Universe in a Grain of Sand*. I bury my head in it, and phrases like *reflect on small things and large; consider the tyranny of your senses* and *observe others closely* fly around in my mind like dazzled birds in a bright sky looking for somewhere to land.

Half an hour and numerous strange ideas, noises and aromas later, Mum comes in with something she says is Hungarian goulash. Why can't she just buy supermarket pizza, I think. I make myself beans on toast for one instead.

'You're so sulky. What's up?' Mum says, burping politely as we eat. 'The footie not go well?'

'Mum, you send your texts too early. The game hadn't even begun and you're telling me *never mind*.'

'But I have to do the shopping after.'

'We lost. I didn't play. I need new boots.'

'We don't have the money for new boots. Anything else?'

She has the money for a new car but not new boots? *WTF*? I storm out.

23

I lie on my bed with the *Philosophy Book* on my lap and reflect. There are two big questions in my life. (1) Will I ever get into the starting line-up of the school football team? (2) Will I ever see my dad?

I imagine my dad as Messi and he comes to watch me play a game. I dribble round all eleven of the opposing team then sock the ball into the net. Messi – aka my dad – runs on to the pitch, crying tears of joy for me. The Windmill declares, 'From today and for ever more, this boy's name shall be the first on the team sheet!' I get a standing ovation from everyone in the crowd and the 1966 England World Cup Team provide my Guard of Honour as the other boys carry me off the pitch like a Roman Emperor.

So much for dreams.

I write my blog.

Match Report by the Reluctant Blogger

The eleven selected players of Hopeless Eleven successfully trotted on to the pitch. There they began colliding with each other, with the goalposts, with the referee and didn't stop colliding for the rest of the match. PS. The substitute was rubbish too. Score: Hopeless Eleven 0: Other Team 9. The Hopeless Eleven coach declared it an improvement on the last match. This is mathematically correct since they lost the last match 0:13.

Mum shouts up. 'There's a film about zombies coming on. Will you watch it with me?'

I shout back down, 'What's it called?'

'I dunno,' she says, 'it's a love story, but with zombies and that. Please! I dropped your sister off at a club earlier and I've only got you for company.'

I go downstairs. I look at her two cats and the kitten spread about the room – aren't they company and what does she get them for if they're not? The film is zombie hikers chasing around a forest biting flesh out of each other. The commercials come on.

'So, Mustapha's gone then?' I ask Mum.

'Yes,' Mum sniffles. 'I couldn't afford him.' She says it as if he's a cat.

'What about Rory? Why did you drop him?'

'My ex-ex? Oh, don't even go there. Whenever I left a room he switched the light off. It got annoying.'

'And your ex-ex-ex?'

'Hilton?'

'Yeah. What was his sin?'

Mum laughs, remembering. 'I have broad musical tastes but I draw the line at *The Bell Ringers of Kwa Zulu*.'

'What's wrong with that?'

'It was like living in Notre Dame. I was becoming Quasimodo. It was all right for you; you were at school – you didn't have to listen.'

'You're no good at relationships, are you, Mum? That's why your photo-frames are all quick release.'

'Very funny, Lenny. Actually, I'm brill. It's the quality of the men out there that's lacking.'

I look around. The living-room clock sits on a spotless mantelpiece above an electric fire that has these propellers inside and a light so it makes shadows that look like flames. If you listen closely it gives off a little hum as the propellers spin round. The walls have brown flock wallpaper with silver strands running through it that the cats like to try to claw out. There are four old-style lamp fittings, one set in each wall, and all of them flicker if you put the kettle on. The floor is new though. Me and Mum fitted eight packs of laminate planks one weekend all on our own, and they look good from all angles except from the front door so Mum makes sure guests don't linger there.

The film's back on and immediately there's chunks of flesh falling out of the sky and the screen coats with blood. Mum hugs me, screaming, which is fun. I watch the zombies chase around for a bit more, then pick up the football book to take it back upstairs and drag myself to bed.

In bed I wonder what my mum means by the quality of the men out there. And what was wrong with my dad that made them split up.

The moon is up in the sky. I hear Mum go to bed, sobbing. I think, That'll teach her to watch zombie films all night. I go into her room, kiss her and say, 'I love you, Mum, you're the greatest.'

'I love you too, sweetie,' she says, then turns her face into the pillow.

In my room, I lie back and try to read, but my mind keeps drifting. I think, my mum's not the only one who could weep. If it wasn't for her, I'd probably have run away. You can get a Megabus ride to anywhere in England for under five pounds.

I catch myself falling asleep, then something jumps on my legs. It's the kitten. I take it downstairs, close the living-room door so it can't get back up, then go to bed again.

I'm snoozing. Floating peacefully in an ocean.

Suddenly there's a clatter downstairs.

Laughter. The door opening. Slamming. Opening again. Stumbling outside.

It's my sister returning from the club. I hear the rattly engine of the taxi fade away. Why does she always have to return at silly o'clock? Mum stays up worrying and then she's too tired to make my breakfast and I have to eat cereal.

The house rumbles again.

Duuurrr.

The noise stops. Another noise now. Higher pitched.

Diiirrr.

Duuurrr Diiirrr.

The two sounds have combined and are looping. The noise is coming from inside my room. Everyone's in bed, asleep. There's only me awake. What is it? I shuffle up in my bed. I can see a shimmer of blue light projecting from one corner of the room – my bookcase. Noiselessly, I slide off the bed. It's louder now.

Duuurrr Diiirrr.

It's the football book. A strange energy shifts around the room as I start to open its cover. The curtains open, then close. Something is happening here. The book lights up.

Duuurrr Diiirrr. Duuurrr Diiirrr.

A footballer lifts himself off the page of the book. His skin is peeling then reforming. His lower jaw loosens from his face then moves silently back into place. I can see the bone of his eye-socket. He fixes me with a look that is indescribably fierce. Then he speaks.

'Zombie power.'

That's all he says.

All these footballs launch at the zombie like they're being fired from a machine. The zombie traps each ball with its knees and shoots it at me. *Smack. Smack. Smack.* I can't catch even one of them, they come at me so fast, so hard. I cry out with pain. The zombie laughs. As it laughs, its whole body breaks up into blue light squares and it's gone as suddenly as it arrived.

The glow of the book fades down until it's just a tiny blue pixel in the middle of the page.

Then nothing.

My whole body tingles.

Next morning, Mum wakes me and says I was sleepwalking in my room last night. Apparently, I had my fists clenched and was shouting, 'Zombie Power!' She says the last time I sleepwalked, I did the same thing – only I was downstairs, kneeling in front of the fridge shouting something random. Sometimes, she says, I scare her.

The Head Teacher announces at Assembly that: 'Someone is undermining the honour of the school with an anonymous blog' and if he finds out who it is, they are in deep trouble. It is not sporting to criticise the team publicly 'since it erodes team spirit'.

Thanks to the Head's announcement, I get nineteen new Followers on my blog.

THE DEAD ARISE

Another Saturday. Another match. All three of us are on the substitutes' bench again.

I say to Eddie, 'There's the living, playing out there on the pitch. And we're the dead, here on the bench. This bench is our twin coffin.'

'Coffin for three.'

'Huh?'

'Sheba.'

'OK. Two boys and a girl.'

'Three boys. Sheba's an honorary boy.'

'What?'

'It means we make an exception for her. Because she's good.'

'Right.'

Sheba leans over. 'Did you just call me exceptional, Eddie?'

'Sort of,' says Eddie.

Sheba pats his knee.

Eddie goes red.

I try to get my head round Eddie's *exception* idea but give up and decide I'll look it up in my *Philosophy Book* later. Sheba and Eddie are hardly talking, just watching the match. It's strange because before Sheba, me and Eddie didn't bother watching – what was the point when we never got to play? Sheba's face moves with every kick of the ball. Her hands flick up and down and her feet shift around. The ball goes out of play near to us and Sheba shoots over to it in a blur of feet and stuffs it into the hands of one of our players.

I nod to Eddie. 'She's Road Runner.'

Eddie chuckles.

The Windmill's pointing her back to the bench. I have an arm-wrestle with her. She's got pretty good biceps for a girl. Eddie plays the winner, which means me, and he easily beats me. Eddie's 99 per cent muscle.

We're playing on a pitch surrounded by fields of long, golden grass. The other team has scored three goals and are doing a group hug in the centre circle. Big deal. They ain't all that. Sheba and Eddie start chatting again. I tug Eddie's shirt.

'I've got three dads – beat that.'

'Whatchutalkinabout?' goes Eddie, rummaging in his nose.

'My Birth Certificate dad, on an oil rig. My stepdad who my mum has swapped for a car. And here's the thing. Gary Lineker's my actual dad.'

'Whatever.'

'Seriously.'

Eddie's not listening but Sheba's sitting at my feet now.

'That's amazing, Lenny.'

'Yeah, Gary Lineker used to be a footballer, you know, for England before he started doing the crisps advert,' I tell her. I pull his pic out of my sleeve. 'Do you see the resemblance? My mum used to work as a cleaner in the

Chelsea VIP area where they drink cocktails. She met him there and he fancied her and they did things.'

'Your mum had sex with Gary Lineker?'

We all laugh again.

'Don't you think I look like him?'

She squints both eyes. 'Apart from the eyes. And the head shape. And the hair colour. And the skin colour. And the nose. Maybe.'

A text from Mum pings into my phone.

Never mind Lenny its the taking part that counts. Love you loads. xxxxMum

Eddie grabs my phone and reads it and he's doubled over laughing. He shows it to Sheba but Sheba doesn't laugh; she says, 'Ah, that's sweet,' and hands my phone back to me.

Sheba's own phone starts ringing. She fishes it out and wanders off to take the call. I feel like stretching my legs so I sort of walk behind her. All I pick up is 'yeh' 'of course' 'no, no, no' and 'I double dare you'.

Suddenly she turns round. 'Are you eavesdropping on me, Leonard Blackwood?'

'Only because you have something stuck on your tracksuit.'

'Take it off then.'

'It's fallen now. It was chewing gum.'

'Ew.'

The Windmill trots over, waving his linesman's flag at us. 'Warm up, warm up!'

Here we go again, I think. The needless warm-up routine. Fifteen minutes left of the game, the pitch is totally churned up, we're playing uphill, and it's hopeless. Sheba does her gymnastics stretchy thing. Eddie does star jumps. I check the laces on my boots.

The Windmill's back. We're down 5:0. 'Make an impact, yeh?' he tells us.

Sheba rockets up and down. 'Pick me, sir, I've been practising my throw-ins all week!'

'Sheba, you're going on for sure. Any throw-ins, you take them. Make them big and close to their goalie. OK boys, for the other substitute it's between you two. To keep it fair, I'm tossing a coin.'

I groan because I'm never lucky. Leonard Blackwood never wins anything.

The coin zooms up into the sky, hangs there a moment, then plummets down and lands in The Windmill's palm. His fingers fold over it fast.

'It's Eddie,' he says. 'Go get 'em, Eddie!'

'Wait a minute,' says Eddie. 'Was it Heads or Tails?'

'Er … Heads,' The Windmill says, impatient.

'Then that's Lenny,' says Eddie. 'Lenny was Heads.'

'Fine,' the coach says, though he's frowning at Eddie. 'It's your lucky day, Lenny. You're on!'

'Zombie Power!' I yell at the top of my lungs.

The referee who has come over to check our boots, laughs. 'Even zombies might not be able to help you lot,' he says. I ignore him because suddenly my boots are buzzing and I need to get on the pitch right this minute. The coach talks to the referee and he allows us one more substitution so Eddie gets to play as well.

I'm on fire. I spring on to the pitch and call for the ball. I leap this way and that but nobody ever passes the ball properly. The other team start attacking. I get a few tackles in but the referee calls them fouls and awards a free kick against us. They score a fluky goal from the free kick. When the game restarts nobody passes me the ball so I push one of our own players off it. I see Rocket on the left wing and whack the ball up to him. He traps it but gets tackled so it's our throw-in. Sheba takes the throw-in. She runs up, does a head-over-heels front flip while holding the ball, and – whoosh – the ball flies through the air, bounces off Eddie's skull and hits the net.

We've scored! Everyone rushes to congratulate Eddie even though it was my kick that started the move off.

The opposing team are on the lookout for me now because I've made a difference. They slam into me time and time again. I slam back into them and they win another two free kicks and then a penalty. The Windmill throws down his linesman's flag in protest but the referee's mind is made up. They score again.

'Calm it down, Lenny, you're making a fool of yourself!' The Windmill shouts.

I'm the only one on our team who's trying to win and I've got one gashed shin, one split head, a shirt full of mud and socks bathed in blood to show for it.

We lose 9:1.

We're trudging back to the changing room when there's a sudden squall. Everyone runs for shelter. I take one last glance back at the pitch – and see on the far side, almost obscured by rain, a lone figure standing with a ball tucked under his arm. It's the zombie from last night. I shudder and run.

In the changing room, under the cobwebs and mould, above the swing and bang of the metal door and the clatter of angry feet, and the double wallop as one of Horse's boots follows the other into the breeze-block walls, the coach is trying to be positive. 'Great throwing, Sheba. And one incredible leap from you, Eddie, like a frog on springs.'

Eddie takes a bow. Sheba's sitting next to him and pats him on the back.

'As for Lenny ...'

Some people are laughing already which I don't understand. The coach holds his hand up for silence. Then he says it.

'It's Fright Night next week – I guess Leonard started early!'

The whole changing room erupts with laughter. *I can take it. I'm bigger than them. The pricks in my eyes are not tears.* Sheba's sitting next to me. She rests her hand on mine for a moment.

'Calm! Calm! Calm!' the coach shouts. There's a hush. 'If you could all have Leonard's energy and application, we'd be at the other end of this league table!'

The coach walks away. I grab my bag and walk out. As I go past the changing-room office, there's a sound coming from inside. It could be the loose wheel on the squeaky office chair that's developed a new sound. Or maybe there's a frog in the big wire bin of spare PE kits. Or some loose chalk rolling at the bottom of the crate of rolled-up flip charts that hold plans for the matches we've lost in the past. But it sounded like sobbing.

'Are you all right, sir?' I call out. The Windmill calls out yes, he's just clearing his throat. Sheba nudges me to walk on. We head out.

'Wow, Lenny, you played your socks off,' says Sheba, 'like you was wearing magic boots!'

I smile. 'I dunno what came over me. I had this d-dream. A zombie talked to me and said I had zombie power and stuff.'

'A zombie?' she whispers.

I'm embarrassed. I don't look at her. 'Yeh.'

'That's so cool. Do you get zombie dreams often?'

'Don't tell Eddie.'

'Don't tell Eddie what?' Eddie's with us now. He's come running up.

'It's a full moon in two days' time and I've got a telescope!' Sheba bursts out. 'We could all go stargazing together. How about it, Lenny?'

'Sounds good to me,' I say, wondering if she's serious.

'Yeh, stargazing,' says Eddie, practising heading an imaginary ball.

We reach the bus stop and we're mobbed. Everybody wants to know how Sheba did that front flip supersonic throw-in. Eddie is the first player to score a goal in five matches so they're practically kissing his feet. Nobody slaps my back for giving the team the energy to score goals. I slide away.

Only Sheba notices. 'Lenny! Wassup?' she calls out.

'I've got things to sort my ends, text me!' I shout to her.

I duck into a corner shop and look around for a drink – all that running on the pitch has dried my throat. I pick up a shadow in the shop – a man in a blood-spatter Halloween T-shirt and bushy black beard who follows me across all three aisles. I turn round and ask him where the drinks cabinets are. He points one out to me at the back then helps me find the fizzy guava juice: it was hidden by a doubled-up row of cola cans.

Outside again, I think about Sheba. She throws the ball further than any boy and it can't be her hands because they're tiny so it has to be the way she throws it. She's like a human catapult. I try remembering how she does it. I can do a front flip – where you run up, tuck in, then do a handstand and rotate round and straighten up. But I can't imagine doing it with a ball in my hands because I use my hands for the push off. Cutting through the park, I have a go at it. I run up using the can as an imaginary ball, but I chicken out of the actual flip. Instead I juggle the empty guava can on my knee the rest of the way home.

Mum complains because my trousers are all ripped at the knees and muddy and says why don't I use the bus fare she gives me and if I'm not going to use it she'll not bother giving it me any more. I wait, dripping sweat on the living-room floor, till she calms down.

All the while, my sister is pulling faces at me behind Mum's back, miming Mum ranting and trying to get me to giggle so I get in even more trouble. This is what I put up with.

Finally, Mum's run out of breath. She sniffs my hair.

'I'm thinking of getting a parrot,' she tells me.

'Don't cats eat birds?' I say.

'Umm, I hadn't thought of that.'

I follow her into the kitchen. She's cooking something she calls mushroom risotto. I watch her stir rice into a bowl of gloop that could be mushy peas and turnips mashed together, mixed with the insides of a chicken. It smells foul. Mum holds out a spoonful for me. It has me heaving up in the kitchen sink. I make a mental note never to eat rice and mushrooms together again ever in my entire life.

Still leaning over the kitchen sink, I get my bearings. There's a cat clawing at my feet because right next to my shoes there's a row of cat-food bowls and the cat's afraid I'll spill some. Across the way, I can see the oven light is on. The oven door has only one glass because the other glass shattered when Carla roller-skated into it, but the oven still works. Mum's put wood panelling on all the kitchen walls, 'so it's more like a Swedish sauna'. The kitchen window doesn't open so it's as hot as a sauna once all the cooking starts.

I take a long drink straight from the kitchen tap then go upstairs. I do my homework, then write my blog:

Hopeless Zombie Eleven Reluctant Blogger Report
There was a ball. There were 22 players and there was a referee. There were also 167 throw-ins, 85 free kicks, 46 offsides, and 15 bags of crisps eaten at half-time. At full-time the score line was 9:1 We lost. Coach said it could have been 11:1 This is technically accurate, but who wants to celebrate 9:1?

I post the Blog then find the *Philosophy Book* and open that. *Be observant of the tiniest things while also thinking the biggest ideas.* It takes me a while to get my head around that one. I decide it means the world is a big place yet it has room for ants.

I find my *Frankenstein* book but it gives me the chills so I stop reading it. I look through my dad's 1966 football book. There's a boy in a crowd photograph who's about eleven. He's wearing a flat cap and a thick, woolly coat and he's waving a wooden rattle, held up in one gloved hand. He's screaming so loud you can count the teeth in his mouth.

His eyes are looking right at the camera as he screams. I imagine being him. He's white and I'm black but we both love football. Maybe we could swap lives if time travel was possible. The players he's screaming at are thundering up the pitch. One of them is airborne. The camera has caught him in a bicycle kick, about to strike the leathery ball.

Mum shouts for me to come and help tidy up. I end up watching another film with her. This time a hooded axe-man is attempting to kill all the people living in a barn in the middle of a wood. The soundtrack is savage howls, as if someone's sawing the leg off a bear.

'What *is* this, Mum?' I quiz her.

'It's a fairy tale, but updated.'

'Which one?'

'*Red Riding Hood*,' she says. 'Don't worry, they all come back alive in the end.'

Only the teenage girl survives the first hour because she's got a special scream which protects her. After about the tenth time the axe-man decapitates someone, I say I'm going to bed.

'You're like a bear,' Mum says, 'always going up to your room.'

In bed I open up my *Philosophy Book*. Under the chapter called *Classical Axioms*, it's got tons of sayings. I memorize a few that, if I said them, would make me sound deeply wise, then I find Dad's football book again. I feel it in my hands, wondering where he bought it and whether he imagined his son would one day read it. His own hands had to have held this book one time, just like my hands are holding it now.

As I look at the picture of the boy holding the rattle, I notice there's a man next to him that could be his dad.

Maybe it could be my dad standing next to me like that one day. The page begins to glow as the boy starts shouting with excitement. The players are rushing after the leathery ball. I stare and stare at the page till the room fades away and I can feel every detail of the photo. The book begins to glow. I feel my body tingling. In place of the cheer of the crowd there's this faint howling, like a bear in pain. The players play on. One of them dashes right to the edge of the page and bursts out into my room.

I drop the book and look at him.

His skin is split. His bones have burst through their flesh. Droplets of blood circle his face.

He has a net filled with footballs slung over his shoulder.

There's a bloodied axe in the net-bag too.

He looks right at me. His lips are shedding skin like a moulting snake. He shouts:

'Zombie power!'

Balls start firing at him from all corners of the room. He traps them and boots them at me in a flurry of volleys. I try to block them, flinging myself this way and that as a bear howls and howls and howls somewhere.

'Zombie power!'

'Wake up!'

Mum's shaking my foot.

'Stop screaming, sweetie, you're frightening Oklahoma.'

I look around me. I'm inside my wardrobe.

Oklahoma is the name she's given to the kitten. I peer out. My sister's in my room too.

'Get out!' I tell Carla.

39

'Hah, he's awake now,' she sneers. She drags her PJ-wrapped bones out of my room.

I get out of the wardrobe. Mum's sniffing my hair again.

'Stop sniffing my hair, Mum.'

She wants to tuck me in but I tell her to leave me alone.

Next day the Head Teacher says well done to the netball team, brilliant news that the new tortoise is finally eating the school lettuce waste, and finally, that people writing critical blogs *Do Not Help the Football Team*.

I get thirty new Followers.

STARS AND SPORES

It's a dark night. We're in a field looking upwards. The soil is warm and dry because it hasn't rained for ages. Above us, the sky soars on and on. There's a sweep of milkiness, but stars everywhere and forever. We're lying on our backs – me, Sheba and Eddie.

'Wow,' goes Sheba.

'True dat,' says Eddie.

'Just wow,' I agree.

I try to count the stars in just one corner of the sky but I can't even start. Some of them switch on and off.

'Whoa,' goes Eddie.

'What?' I look where he's pointing.

'This whoosh thing, it shot across – *voom* – like that, then disappeared – *ping*.' He clicks his finger to show how fast it disappeared.

'That's a shooting star,' says Sheba. 'I didn't see. Eddie, lend me your glasses.'

'Here.'

'Oh-oh-oh!' goes Sheba.

'Are you OK?' I ask. She sounds ill.

She sighs. 'I think I've died and gone to heaven.'

'Yeh, it's beautiful,' says Eddie. 'A fairy tale in the sky, with stars.'

It's the most poetic thing I've heard Eddie say. There's a tree with only a few little leaves left on the edge of the field that's partly in our view of the sky so I know what he means about fairy tale.

I take a breath. 'Doesn't it scare you?' I ask them.

'What do you mean?' Eddie says.

'The stars are so far away.'

'And?' He doesn't get it.

'How old the Universe is. We're only around for a second.'

He gets it now. 'Scary,' says Eddie.

'Let's hold hands,' says Sheba.

Her fingers are warm and soft.

'It feels like the stars are less cold now,' I tell her.

'I want my glasses back,' says Eddie. Then, 'I need to pee.' He gets up. 'Keep looking that way, I'll take two big steps.'

'Go further,' Sheba tells him. 'We don't want your pee blowing on us.'

'It's dark though.'

'Use your phone light.'

'Uh, right. Don't look.'

Sheba's hand tightens around mine. We can hear Eddie having a trickly piddle. Sheba's silently laughing. It does sound funny.

'We're all made of stardust,' I say. I read it in the *Philosophy Book*.

'Even Eddie?'

Eddie comes clumping back and trips over us. 'Duke of Edinburgh finishes at eight and it's eight now,' he says.

That is the evening class we're supposed to be attending. He shows us the clock on his phone.

'Sheesh,' says Sheba, 'we'd better get going.'

We scramble up.

Eddie and Sheba get though the gap in the hedge on to the road. I'm about to squeeze through when a big shadow of a man comes running up and stops me. 'You! Get back, get back!'

I stumble back into the field. He's on the high ground because the field drops from the road. I can only see his silhouette at first, because he's in front of the street light. He has one bony fist raised, like he might punch me.

'What're you doing here?' he asks.

My eyes adjust. He's thin, with lank, grey hair like two curtains and wearing a dark pullover and Army trousers. His chest jerks from having run up. His skin is flaky white. He could be a zombie.

'We've been looking at the stars,' I tell him, watching carefully to see what he does with the fist and if his face starts peeling.

'Or stealing my chickens. Gimme your bag.'

I take my school bag from my shoulder slowly. He grabs it. It holds my school books and a football. He shakes it about, rummages his fist hand in it. Finally, he accepts what I told him. His face looks stiff with disappointment.

'If I find any dead chickens in this field tomorrow morning, I'll be calling at your school with the police. In fact …' Next thing, this phone light comes on in his fist and I hear the shutter click. 'Evidence,' he says. 'Now get off my land!' He steps aside and watches every move I make through the field hedge.

I run like hell away from him.

'What was that about?' says Eddie, running up to me with Sheba.

'Just some weirdo with beef about chickens.'

'Nutter!' Eddie yells into the darkness.

We look but nothing and no one emerges out of the gloom. A fog is starting to lie down. We wander into it.

'It's not a farmer's field,' goes Eddie.

'What is it then?' asks Sheba.

We're walking in a line, our shoes hitting the ground at the same time. Sheba's glittery ones, Eddie's thick leather shoes, and my blue trainers. The main road is in two turns.

'It's a flood field. For when the river overflows.'

'What river?' Sheba says.

'I dunno.'

We listen out for a river but we don't hear one.

The bus comes on time and I make it home for about 8.30 p.m.

'How was the Duke of Edinburgh?' Mum asks from the kitchen. I've flung my bag down and kicked off my trainers.

'Brilliant,' I say 'we're learning knots.'

I'm surprised how easily the lie flew off my tongue. I sniff the air. I'm hungry from all those stars.

Mum's come into the living room now. 'You enjoyed it then?'

'Reef knots, gate knots, lasso knots – millions of knots. It's well cool, Mum, you should see …'

'Tell me another time,' says Mum, stifling a yawn, which is fine by me. Then, 'What's all that grass on your back?'

Mum's in that mood where she's just asking questions and you don't need to actually answer them. She goes through the kitchen to the back yard where she lights up a cigarette. Mum tries to hide her smoking but you can always smell it on her afterwards even if you don't glimpse her at the back door with an orange glow round one of her hands. She comes back in.

'I've made you a stuffed eggplant.'

'Mum. What even is it?'

'Try it, you might like it. I watched the TV chef Gordon Ramsay. But I added my own twist. Go on, try it.'

It's not that bad and I feel I should do something good after having lied about Duke of Edinburgh so I force myself to swallow the entire plateful. I'm almost finished when the door goes *rapa tap … tap*. I know the sound instantly.

'Mustapha's here, Mum!' I call out.

'There's a surprise,' says Mum, but she's already put some lippy on so I know she was expecting him. My sister's not in else I would have looked across at her and she would have squinted her eye to tell me Mum was up to something. I notice his photo's back in the quick release photo-frame.

Mustapha bowls in wearing a ridiculous brown uniform with 'We Deliver' in a big yellow circle on the back of the jacket. 'Hello, Lord Leonard,' he says, holding out his hand stiffly like we're two members of the Royal Family.

I nod and carry on eating the eggplant. He parks himself on the sofa, next to me and looks at the TV.

'What's this then?' he calls out to Mum.

'*Night of the Hollow Dead*!' she yells to him from the kitchen. She comes out with another eggplant.

'Oh eggplant – my favourite,' he says, which is what he says whatever she gives him. Then of the film: 'The zombies win, don't they?'

'You like zombie films?' I ask him.

'Not really, but this one's dead good … Get it? "Dead good"?'

This is what I have to put up with.

'How's the new job been?' Mum asks, sitting next to him, stroking his jacket, letting him know she's impressed. Mustapha budges up, which crushes me into an even smaller space. I'll soon be sitting on the arm of this thing, I think. Why doesn't Mum sit on one of the chairs?

Mustapha shakes his hair and puffs out his chest. 'It's not easy, Julie. It's a highly skilled job. You've got the yellow boxes, the green boxes, the white ones. And you've got to sort each of the dockets alphabetically and then geographically by zone, and then chronologically by the route. After you've done that …'

Mustapha drones on and on and on. I can't believe Mum is still listening to it, but she is, like it's live commentary of a World Cup Final. Mustapha has this two-tone beige-brown skin with thick black bristles that erupt fast along the middle of his cheeks, slow at the chin, then fast again along the neck. When he smiles, they all dance upwards except the ones at the middle of his chin where the dimple is – those ones turn into each other. I realize I know Mustapha's face better than I know my own dad's face. I know the postman's face better as well. Mustapha's stuffing himself with the stuffed eggplant. It doesn't slow down his talking.

'… if the reverse warning light fails in that case you have to do a three-point turn …'

I can't take any more. 'Mum, can you ask him to be quiet? I'm trying to watch the film.'

'What about your homework?'

'I did it at Duke of Ed. They help you with it.'

Mustapha continues yammering, this time about how back-breaking and exhausting the job of driving a delivery van is, on a par with coal mining.

'You poor thing, having to do all that. Go and have a rest upstairs,' Mum says kindly.

'Is he staying overnight?' I ask.

Mustapha's stopped his tired man's roll up the stairs. He wants to hear the answer too.

'He won't be using your toothbrush, if that's what you're worried about,' Mum says.

'Sorry about that,' Mustapha says down to me, then, 'Yeah, sorting those boxes, lifting them, I'm dead beat.' He continues up the stairs with his fake weary legs.

The stuffed eggplant sits like lead in my stomach. I don't move in case I either throw up or something goes wrong at the other end.

My sister gets back and enters the room how my sister enters any room. Big cloud of perfume. Words falling everywhere. Hugs. Shopping bags strewn across everything that doesn't move. A quick dance on the rug.

'Spill it, what's happened, our Carla?' Mum asks.

Carla gushes how she's been offered this amazing opportunity by a Festival to make these walkabout costumes for them and they do festivals all over Europe so if they like the costumes and they perform well she could take some real money and travel all over Europe and so she has to start designing them, like now, right now.

'No good ideas ever come off an empty stomach,' Mum says, slapping a bowl of microwaved eggplant in front of her.

'This is … yummy,' Carla declares. She eats it all off in thirty seconds and sits on the sofa sketching. She nudges me. 'You shouldn't watch this, it'll give you nightmares.'

I want to give her a *what's-it-to-you?* look but a little bubble of indigestion works though me and I end up looking at her like a stunned fish, then burp.

She gives me her *if-I-could-swap-you-for-a-tin-of-cat-food-I-would* smile.

In the film, the zombies are in a graveyard rooting around for something. Various graves erupt, flinging up bones. The camera zooms in on one. A moss-covered slab of stone lifts and there's an underground scuffling sound. A hand emerges which is not all bone, but close. It's greenish and blood-speckled. Another hand. The camera creeps round the side. The eerie music gets loud over the scraping and ripping sounds. A deep sucking noise picks up, faster and faster. *Dirrr. Dirrr. Suck. Suck. Sucksucksuck*. Then the slab itself is flung away, the ground heaves and …

The TV cuts to a commercial break.

I find myself holding my sister's hand. She hasn't noticed. I slowly edge my hand free.

'Did you see the sky this evening?' I ask her.

'Were the stars out?' She's sketching a costume of some sort.

'Constellations and everything.'

'I might pop my head out then. What d'you think?' She shows me her sketch.

'Is it the right way round?'

She snatches it back. 'It's an amoeba.'

'Huh?'

48

'Never mind, lickle brother, my art is too sophisticated for juvenile minds.'

There's clumsy footsteps upstairs in the bathroom.

'Is that Mo?' Carla immediately asks.

'He's stopping over.'

'Oh. That's why Mum's plucked her eyebrows.'

'What?'

'Never mind. Let me measure you.'

I have no choice in the matter. Carla stands me up and runs a tape measure all around me.

'Who've you been rolling in the grass with?' she says, turning me round.

'I was looking at the stars.'

'Yeah, right.'

She's done with measuring me and then the film's back on so I shush her.

It's dark like the vastness of space. A sound comes from an unknown hollow. *Thuck. Thuck.* The soundtrack grows. The screen is black then becomes spores – almost pretty – soft, hooked pink spores. The camera pulls back a little. The spores are swimming in an eye that has a festering, gangrenous eyelid. This eyelid heaves up and then two eyes throb, both brimming with spores, and speckled with blood. The camera crawls across the face to show a thistle-haired nose. Then, in one big heave: *the whole of a zombie face shoots right out of the screen.*

Carla screams. 'Turn it off! Turn it off!'

Thuck. Thuck. The soundtrack keeps running.

Upstairs, Mustapha is laughing. I can hear a buzz from up there which means he's using my toothbrush again as I am the only one with an electric toothbrush in this house.

49

Mum comes in from the back. She's had another cigarette. 'What's the matter?' she asks Carla.

'Nothing. I stabbed myself with a needle.'

Mum settles herself into the sofa with us. I don't understand. There's spare chairs everywhere.

'So, you and Mo back together then?'

Mum sighs at Carla. 'The devil you know – you know?' she whispers.

Carla laughs into her sketch.

I try to get them to stop but they go into this girl-talk that is as endless as the Universe and pulls all subjects into it like a black hole, from how to superglue windscreen wipers to the origin of Arabian horses. Finally, Mum says, 'I'm really tired, I guess I'll have an early night.'

'Try to keep the noise down,' Carla says to her.

Mum smiles. 'I'll whack him if he starts snoring.'

Carla raises another eyebrow.

Later, I'm on my own in my bedroom, at my window, looking at the stars in the sky. I know I'm Aries, the Ram, but I can't make it out anywhere. I also know Libra the Scales, Cancer the Crab, and Leo the Lion. I can't see any of them even though I look until my eyes are sore.

I give up and find the football book. There's this photo of a player who's just kicked the ball and it's soaring up into the sky. I look and look into the photo. Slowly, it becomes 3D. I feel my body tingling. The pitch, the stands, the crowd, the players, all come alive. I step inside the scene and gaze up into its sky. Then this real eeriness starts. The footballers stop playing and one by one start looking upwards with me. Slowly, the stars begin to arrange themselves. They're pulsing. It's as if some hugely powerful magnet is shifting the stars around.

The pulsing becomes stronger. Clusters of stars form. Shooting stars trace between the clusters and it's then that an indescribably bright image writes itself into the sky. It's a face. *The face of a zombie.* The zombie face surges forwards till it fills my vision. There's a high-pitched whirling sound in the air. Then a disembodied voice calls out: 'Zombie power!'

My lips move automatically. 'Zombie power.'

Suddenly the zombie face shoots back into the far sky and starts aiming stars at me. To protect myself, I hold out my hands. The stars bounce off my palms. One gets through and tears into my skin. I cry out at the burning pain.

'Wake up this minute!'

'Wake!'

I open my eyes. Someone's shaking me. The skin of a beetle. The voice of my mum.

My cheek stings.

'Wake!'

Another sting.

'Up!'

Mum. The coils of her hair twisting and turning.

I stare up at her, wondering why she's over me and looks like she's going to slap me. Behind her is my sister.

'Trying to get in touch with ET?' Carla says.

'Take your hand down, sweetie,' Mum tells me, her voice suddenly soft. She's pulling at one of my hands.

But the sky. 'Zombie power.'

Mum's crying. 'This is too much. What if he'd opened the window?' she says to Carla.

I'm drifting awake.

'Go to bed, Mum,' I tell her.

She tucks me into my bed, making the quilt extra tight so I can hardly lift my ribcage to breathe let alone move my body.

Mustapha's holding my mum in his arms. Everyone's looking at me like I'm a specimen under a microscope.

'Get out!' I tell them. I groan.

THE GHOSTS OF 66

'Mum, if I score a goal and everyone comes up to hug me and that everyone includes a girl … Mum, are you even listening?'

Mum is on her knees by the washing machine trying to free some clothes that are stuck in the drum. 'Yeh, go on,' she says, reaching for a spanner on the floor with her hand. I nudge it to her with my toe.

'And that everyone includes Sheba and she comes running up and hugs me as well because I score a goal …'

'Ooh. Did you score a goal?' Mum says in between grunts of effort into the kitchen's rubber floor as she yanks away at the washing-machine's base.

'Mum, listen – and everyone else on the team says I'm gay because I let her hug me for more than three seconds. Why does that make me gay?'

Mum hardly looks up. 'I don't know. Are you gay? I'll love you all the same if you are, wouldn't matter one bit to me. Your Uncle Robbo is gay and he can fly a helicopter.'

She gets up, presses a washing-machine button. The washing-machine door swings open. She's happy. I follow her into the living room.

'No, I'm not, Mum. You're not listening, you didn't even hear my question.'

'What question?'

'See? Oh God, nobody understands me!'

Mustapha looks up. He's in the living room kneeling by an electrical socket with a screwdriver in his hand. It must be Fix It Friday.

'I heard you,' Mustapha says, 'and I understand. It's because they're jealous that the girl likes you, that's why. Simple. So, do you like this girl then?'

'Yes. No. Who are you to be asking me that question?'

'Sorry, my mistake,' goes Mustapha and turns back to the socket.

'Hormones,' Mum loud-whispers to him. She's now typing into a job application form, her face a millimetre from the screen. She needs glasses.

Mum's impossible. I know all about hormones and it's not that – Mum just uses it as an excuse when she doesn't want to make an effort to understand me. I'm thirteen and she still treats me like a child. I'm exasperated. I'm about to stride out and slam the door behind me but I can just imagine Mum turning to Mustapha and saying, 'Told you so'.

So I don't give her the satisfaction. Instead, summoning as much calmness and *philosophical attitude* as I can, I walk, in a dignified manner, to the door.

'Do you need to go to the toilet, love?' Mum says, looking at me.

'Oh God!' I slam the door then dash upstairs and grab my football boots and my book.

As I stomp back down, Mum shouts, 'Get out right now, you little brat. You almost made me delete my application!'

'Stuff your application!' I tell her. I slam the front door after me. I wish I could slam the pair of them out of my life.

I think about it and realize Mum always does these snarky jokes at me when Mustapha's there. She wants to drive me out so it's just her and Mustapha. She could simply ask instead of teasing me. I don't actually mind having Mustapha around if he makes Mum happy. Mum and him have been going out off and on for about nine months now which is a record for Mum. Her boyfriends usually only last two months.

The path I'm on looks over the park. It's got a football playing-field and some smashed-up play equipment in one corner, the rest is grass. Right now, it's deep in metre-high fog that sits only over the park. A few cars speed past. I hear a dog do a long howl, followed by a short yelp.

The temperature outside is too low for old people and their car-washing and hedge-cutting but the cold's got no chance of getting me. Mum bought me a Parka coat and it's as cosy as sitting on a radiator. I breathe out little clouds. I open the football book and look at a photo. They used to play in all sorts of weather, even fog. There's this photo of an old football ground and the players are coated in mud.

As I read the caption below the photo, I feel this tingling. I start to notice something going on out of the corner of my eye. What I thought was droplets of mist dissolving and reforming is actually human shapes. If I look head on, the shapes disappear so I have to kind of *not* look at them – look at them sideways to see them, as if they're a mirage or a shape in clouds or a dream that you're aware you're dreaming. Slowly I work out there's a whole mob of football players out there on the pitch. *And they're not human:* they run solidly and their shouts and tackles and the ref's whistle sound solid. *Yet you can see through them. Their skin floats around their flesh in the way of moulting snake skin.*

One of them whacks the ball really hard and it rolls right up to my feet. It's an orange thing made of leather. I tap it with my toes. It's heavy. In two taps I've got it up in the air. I pivot on my left leg and flight it with my right foot directly to the chest of the player who comes running up. The air goes out of my lungs when I realize who this phantom is. I know him from the book. It's the famous Bobby Charlton. His skin is peeling. One second he looks solid, the next he has no skin at all covering his flesh, like a laboratory corpse. He's wearing the red England kit he wore when he helped to win the World Cup in 1966. He chests the ball down and traps it under his foot.

'Not bad, lad, you weighted that ball exactly right.'

'Who are you all?' I ask him.

'The '66 team.'

'Never!'

'Lads, over here!' he shouts, waving to the other players.

One by one the players come forward and stand on the touchline right in front of me. Men with skin that peels and reforms, solid yet ghost-like. I look down at my book and then up at them. It is the England 1966 World Cup Final Team. Every one of them. Except one. I point to him.

'Who's that?'

'Jimmy. Jimmy Greaves.'

'Huh?'

'You don't recognize our Jimmy because he didn't play in the Final. Broke his heart, it did. We want to play

56

one last Final, with Jimmy as centre forward instead of Geoff Hurst. Geoff doesn't mind, he's here as well, doing the refereeing.' A figure comes out of the mist. It's Geoff Hurst in a black referee kit. The World Cup hero himself.

'You can help us get into a Final. We've chosen you,' says the Geoff Hurst zombie. His skull becomes a fleshed-out, ordinary skin-and-hair-covered head, then flickers back to being a skull again.

'Why me?' I ask him.

'Only the substitute of a team that has lost, lost and lost again would be desperate enough to want a bunch of old zombies like us to help them out. We're just going to finish our training. Join in if you like.'

'Wait,' I call out. I don't understand anything he's saying. I watch them as they go through their training routines and eventually they let me join in. We keep at the same thing time and time again. Every so often one of them shouts something at me like: 'See? Keep your eyes open when you head the ball!' Or, 'Stay on your feet, don't lunge!' Someone crosses a ball to me. I turn and wallop it back.

'No, no, no!' One of the zombies comes over. 'Not like that. You're going at it too fast. Eyes on the ball. Turn. Pivot. Watch. Easy. Have another go!'

He throws the ball at me and I do the move, slower, keeping my eyes glued to the ball. Easy. He throws the ball again and again and I go running along the touchline volleying it back to him.

I'm about to do another volley when this dog comes bounding at me, snarling, trailing a long chain that disappears back into the mist. I'm petrified and cower as it hurls itself at me. The dog jolts to a stop. It's a wide-jawed pit bull. The owner comes into view through the fog. He's big and squat like the dog and laughing. He slips the chain off the neck of the dog then goads the dog on. 'Dinner!' he says to it, pointing at me. The dog runs up and leaps for me. I've got no chance. I scream.

Mid-air, as it's about to bite into my throat, it twists, then drops to the ground, whimpering. I felt vibrations in the ground. Two of the zombies have run up behind me. The dog looks at them, terrified, then bolts into the fog, leaving its owner shouting for it to come back.

I return on to the pitch, walking backwards slowly, listening in case I hear panting again.

'Don't worry about that dog, kid,' one of the zombies says. 'It won't be back any time soon.'

I'm about to start on sliding tackles when I hear someone at the touchline calling my name. I turn.

It's Mustapha. He's banging his gloves together and shivering. He's shrunk his neck into his coat so it looks like his head is screwed straight on to his shoulders. He's doing a lot of blinking. He looks different.

'Freezing out here. What you doing?' he says, waving me over.

'Playing football.'

'Who with?'

'These.'

'These who?'

'The … zombies,' I say. I look around. Suddenly I can't see them.

Mustapha looks around too. 'There's no one else here.'

I shrug.

'Playing with the zombies, eh?' He puts a hand on my shoulder. 'Your mum wants you back inside.'

'She kicked me out five minutes ago.'

'You've been gone two hours. You make me laugh sometimes, Lenny, you know that? You spend your time in a totally different world to the rest of us.'

'What happened to your eyebrows?' I ask him. Close up, he doesn't seem to have eyebrows any more.

'Oh that? I was fixing that socket and it shorted. Burnt off the hairs on my hand as well. It'll save on manicures.'

Mustapha runs his hand across the front of his face as if checking to see if anything else was burnt off. We're almost back home now.

'Why's the house all dark?'

'She's at the shops buying candles.'

Me and Mustapha sit in the semi-dark, lit only by our phone screens. Without eyebrows running across it, Mustapha's face looks like a moonscape. He sees me looking and wiggles his forehead for me. It's almost funny.

I text Sheba.

Am in absolute darkness. Mums bf killed all our electrics.

She texts back with a line of emojis. ☺☹☹

Carla's keys open the door and she comes into the living room with her phone light on, bends down by the coat hooks, opens a box and whacks a switch. All the lights jump back on. 'You two ever heard of a fuse box?' she says. Then, 'Where's Mum?'

'Out buying candles,' Mustapha tells her sheepishly.

Carla sighs. 'She's gone shopping to the nineteenth century?'

An hour later, Mum comes bustling in with a raw chicken, a bag of other shopping and a box of tall white candles that look like maybe she's borrowed them from a church. I can smell she's had a cig on the way too. She groans, 'I was looking forward to lighting these. It would have been so romantic.' She looks across at Mustapha. I imagine my mum and Mustapha over a candle-lit dinner and shudder.

'Right,' says Carla, 'and meanwhile everything in the freezer would have defrosted, that chicken would not get cooked and I couldn't sew my costumes that are due out tomorrow on walkabout.'

'Still,' says Mum, unbothered by Carla's cold water, 'it would have been nice.'

She catches my eye and wags a finger in my direction. 'Did I have something to say to you?'

'You can remember it another time,' I tell her.

'No, I've got it now. Where did you get to? I was worried.'

'The thing is,' I begin, trying to think up a lie quickly.

Mum smells the lie. 'No, I'm not having it. Mo, did you find him? Where was he?'

'In the park, having a kick around.'

'With?'

If I could kick Mustapha to shut up, I would.

'With his … er, mates?'

He's a rubbish liar. He hesitated too long and Mum is on it.

'What mates?'

'His … er, zombie mates. Playing with them. Yeh.'

'Are you having a laugh?' Mum says, and then before he can answer she asks me: 'Is that right?'

There's nowhere for me to go with this conversation. If I say no, Mustapha's going to mouth off. If I say yes, Mum's going to do one.

'Thanks, Mustapha,' I mutter.

I watch Mum's face. She's either going to shout or cry. 'This has got to stop. It's off the scale,' she begins.

Carla saves the day. 'He likes zombies. Big deal,' she says from behind her sewing machine. 'All kids his age are into it. It's Halloween – take a chill pill, Mum. And get that chicken in the kitchen, the bag's leaking blood.'

Mum pulls out of her tailspin. Mustapha shrugs a *sorry-I-messed-up* look at me. I glower at him but forgive him because he actually looks like he's sorry.

'Now, lickle brother …'

'I'm not doing it.'

'Five pounds.'

'What do I do?'

'You and a friend want to wear a costume each for me at a Festival in the city centre tomorrow? The organizer's double-booked and I need two ragamuffins to wear costumes.'

'Ten.'

'Only if you find a friend who'll wear the other one. They have to be lively – be ready to jump about in them.'

I don't have to think one second longer after Carla says the word 'lively'.

I phone Sheba and try to explain to her but it comes out garbled so I hand the phone over to my sister and the two of them have a conversation that goes on so long that by the time she passes me back my phone, two things have happened. (1) all my phone credit is gone. (2) Mum's cooked dinner – she's serving chicken in wine sauce.

'You'll have to buy me more credit,' I tell Carla when she finally hands me my phone back.

'You'll be pleased to know your friend Sheba has got you a pay-rise. It's now fifteen pounds for the day. I spoke to her mum as well and she's OK with it.'

'I still want phone credit though.'

'OK, OK, I'll get you more credit. Deal?'

We bump fists on it. Mum serves everyone chicken in wine sauce. I give everything tainted by the sauce to Carla in exchange for Carla's chicken. Mustapha and Carla like the sauce-poisoned stuff, so everyone's happy.

'Three satisfied customers,' says Mum, standing in the middle of the living room, beaming.

'What's that little blue light wiggling away behind your leg?' Carla asks Mum.

We all look. Nobody sees anything.

'Don't you start,' says Mum. 'I've got enough with Leonard.'

Everyone laughs, including me.

Carla gets busy on her sewing machine. She's going to be up all night finishing the second costume. Mum clears the plates and I help her carry them into the kitchen. She washes and I dry. She's happy because she's finished three different job applications. In the middle of washing the dishes, she hugs me and smells my hair.

'Guess what, Lenny?' she says.

'What?'

'I've got an interview tomorrow.'

'That's great, Mum. Well done.'

She kisses my head.

I go to bed and read my football book. I can hear the *zzzz zzzz* of Carla's sewing machine. It makes me think of how the footballers must have run when the ground had frost on it. Brushing through the frozen grass leaves. *Zzz z zzzz.* I hear my radiator ticking as it cools. And a very faint shouting from beyond my window. It's a football match. Who would play a match at this hour?

The zombies.

I slide out of bed, dress as noiselessly as possible then ease open my bedroom window latch. The big pipe from the bathroom is right alongside my window. Slowly I reach for it, shift my weight and slip my way down. I make it to the kitchen window height. I'm about to jump off into the back garden when I see Mustapha. He's at the window in his PJs, drinking a glass of water. He jumps out of his skin when he sees me. I put a finger to my mouth. *Shh.* He copies me.

I run for the park. The zombies are playing a game in the mist. You can hear grunts as tackles go in, gasps as they chase up the pitch, rips as sliding boots cut through frosty grass. Every so often, their big leather ball heaves up into the air and is caught in the street lights. Someone boots the ball hard. It zooms towards me. I trap it. I'm about to swish my leg to wallop it back to them when there's the thud of a hand on my shoulder.

'Watching the zombies again are we?'

Mustapha.

In a dressing gown.

And no shoes.

I let him lead me back home. He sneaks me up the stairs.

I'm drifting off to sleep when there's this huge blue flash everywhere in the room. I hear Carla scream like someone's torn out her insides. I try to scream myself but I can't breathe in enough.

I'm trapped in my bed.

HYPNOTIC

I go downstairs in the morning to find Mum chain-smoking in the living room.

'Mum,' I tell her, 'you're not supposed to!'

'Our Carla nearly died last night,' she says.

I look across at Carla. She's sitting fast asleep in her sewing-machine chair. She looks dead. Only the tremor of one of her frizzes of hair near her nose tells me she's breathing. She has one hand on a needle and thread, the other on her phone.

'What happened?' I ask Mum.

'Didn't you hear the bang?'

I shake my head.

'You'd sleep through the end of the world, you would.' She tugs on her cigarette then continues: 'It's not Mo's fault. Ever since I had Maximum Bob fit the Victorian gas-lights, the electrics have been funny. Mo thinks Bob sliced though a cable – he's gone to get an electrician. I told him no Sparks is setting foot in my house again unless he can show me his Certificate.'

Some say Maximum Bob has that name because he gives you the maximum amount of time to pay his loan.

Carla says it's because he charges you the maximum interest he can get away with.

As if by thinking about someone, you can summon them, Carla snores her final snore, shifts a cat off her arm and starts stretching and grunting.

'And what were you climbing out of the window for last night?' Mum squint-eyes me.

Eh? I don't know what she's talking about.

'"Watching the zombies play football in the park." You couldn't make it up.'

Mum sucks extra-long on her cigarette, taking clouds and clouds of smoke into her lungs.

'Well, tell the zombies from me, Lenny,' she snarls, exhaling the entire giant cloud of smoke into my face then looking me dead in the eye the way she does before a long rant: 'No son of mine is climbing out of my windows to watch ghosts play football. Even if they are the bleeding 1966 World Cup football team. I've a good mind to write to that Bobby Charlton himself.'

She takes another furious drag of her ciggie. 'Or call an exorcist. God give me strength.' She's burnt through the entire cigarette.

Carla starts coughing and scratching her armpits.

'Sorry, Carla,' Mum goes. 'You all right, love?'

Carla wakes the way Carla always wakes. Grumpily. 'What do you flipping care? You're killing me with that smoke – I've got asthma in case you've forgotten!'

'And a good morning to you too,' Mum mutters. She opens the doors to the living room to air it out then heads upstairs.

Because Mum's left all the doors open, it's soon freezing.

'Are you OK?' I ask Carla, 'Mum said …'

'I'm fine. Look, all the wiring in here, it's dangerous. That flipping Maximum Bob put the lights on the socket circuit and God knows what else. Don't touch any sockets, OK? Else you're toast. All those times you've been sat there watching TV, never mind me, you could have been electrocuted to death. My lickle brother.'

She kisses me on the forehead as she wanders to the kitchen, which is a bit strange because she hasn't kissed me for, like, years. Her breath is pongy.

She's back with a bowl of cornflakes in her hand. 'Now, lickle brother, I had to sew the second one by hand, owing to the power cut, but they're both ready.'

'What's ready?'

'The costumes. You haven't forgotten? I'm paying you and your friend Sheba top dollar to run around in them at the Festival today. We've got …' she checks her phone … 'fifty minutes. Sheba's meeting us there. Where's Mum?'

Mum drives us into the city centre. She's got a Nicorette nicotine patch on each arm and she still asks if it's OK for her to smoke as she drives. Carla gives Mum a look that would freeze the sun.

Mum changes gears. 'I was only asking.'

Our car beetles through the city-centre traffic. Mum knows all the short cuts and how to avoid roadworks, but even so Carla's worried we're going to be late. Mum whacks on some music to chill Carla and it works. She nods along to this Brazilian beat Mum likes.

I'm wedged in the back seat between Fu-Fu and Chi-Chi, which are the names Carla's chosen for her two giant amoeba costumes. They look like pond-life, magnified a thousand times and coloured in, with bits sewn on to them. There's five holes – for the limbs and the head of the wearers. I haven't tried one on yet as we had no time. I'm not sure they're going to cause a sensation like a human Slinky would, or a Human-to-Car Transformer robot, but it's Carla's first booking and I'm going to do my best for her. If it works and she makes enough money, she might go on a European tour, then I'd get her room, which is way, way bigger than mine.

Mum puts the car's heaters on.

'It's hot in here already, Mum,' Carla protests.

'To cool the engine,' Mum explains.

Why heating the inside of the car would cool the engine I don't understand, but I long ago stopped trying to understand Mum's 'new' car – ever since Mum asked me to rock it a bit so she could get it in reverse gear.

'Really?' says Carla.

Mum replies that Kung Fu Ian did the MOT for her and it's taxed, legal and insured and they'd snatch her hand off for it if she put it on eBay because it's a limited edition.

'Yeah, very limited,' Carla smirks.

The front row of the car then goes back to lip-synching to some screechy, old-time band called the Marvelettes.

This is what I have to put up with.

I take stock of my situation. In a death-trap car, sandwiched between two outsize amoeba named Fu-Fu and Chi-Chi while two tone-deaf members of your family shake and bob their talentless Afros to an inane song from a long-ago era. My entire life is this on eternal repeat.

'Cheer up, Lenny, it might never happen,' Mum calls out over the song and in between her off-key warbling.

'Big grins today, OK?' yells Carla in similar style. She shows me all her teeth, like I'm a horse doctor or something.

I am saved from these people by arrival at our destination.

Boar's Head bus station is used mainly by inter-city coaches. Mum parks up and within thirty seconds I see the shape of an arm-waving figure approaching. I point her out. 'Here's Sheba.'

'Just the girl!' says Carla, laughing.

Sheba's towing what looks like her mum behind her. Carla stops from dragging the amoeba out of the back seat and says hello to Sheba and Co. Sheba's looking at the costumes in the car.

'Fantabulous,' she says to me. 'Huggadorious! Which one's mine?'

I'm about to tell her when she gets called over to where her mum and Carla are talking.

'Sabbi, there's to be no running off. You have to stay together with Leonard at all times. And no being rude. I'll be shopping all day in town so you never know if I'll be watching you to see if you're behaving. I promised Mum.'

I realize it must be her sister, not her mum.

'Okaaay,' says Sheba, annoyed at being told off in public before she's even done anything wrong. 'Enjoy the film with your boyyy-friend!'

Sheba's sister goes red and mutters something at Sheba. I don't hear it but whatever she said could cut the ear off an elephant.

Carla's smiling sweetly at everyone, trying to head off the argument so she's not short-staffed. 'Everything will be fine – I'll be watching them like a hungry hawk. Now into the costumes, you two sweeties.'

Mum's driven off to avoid getting a parking ticket. The costumes are leaning on a pane of bus shelter glass like two outsize sugar lumps. I climb into Chi-Chi by attacking the fold in the middle with my limbs. Sheba climbs into Fu-Fu. The material that makes up the leggings and the arms is a kind of nylon that behaves like stretchy cheese. There's a white beret-hoodie that flips over our heads so only the front of our faces shows. Then the white gloves. All set. Sheba puts hers on back to front so Carla has to help her clamber out and do it all again.

'I thought your name was Sheba?' I say, as all this twisting is going on.

'Sabbi's my Punjabi nickname. Sarbjit's my full name and Sheba's the name I chose for myself.'

'Cool. Is your sister really going to meet her boyfriend?'

Sheba nods. 'I saw the tickets in her bag.'

'I thought she was going to strangle you. What did she say?'

'"Wait till you get home, I'm going to … wring you out like a pair of old knickers! *Teri pagal bhena ko leke!*"'

I laugh. I love it when Sheba switches languages.

'Don't worry,' she says. 'Once she's all loved up from seeing her b.f. she'll totally forget about it. Mum will be ringing her to remind her to pick me up: *"Teri pagal bhena ko leke ana, varna wo pura sher mei nachegi!"*'

I laugh as she pretends to be her mum. The way Sheba says it, it's like her mum's hair is on fire and she's slapping the fire out while cursing Sheba at the same time.

Carla finally gets round to describing what we're actually meant to do. 'You take these leaflets to the middle of the Square over there with me. Then jump up and down on the spot shouting, "Love your life! Gobble your germs!" and hand out the leaflets.'

I take one and read it. It's all about a disinfectant that kills the germs that raw chicken carries. Salmonella. There's nothing about amoeba on it at all. I confront my sister. 'We're a pair of germs, aren't we?'

'You are an interesting form of microbe.'

'That has to be disinfected against?'

Sheba whoops. 'Germs! I love them! Let's do this! Let's get this world disinfected! Yeh!' She bounds off into the middle of the Square so fast Carla can hardly catch up with her.

'Not yet,' Carla tells her, panting and bleary-eyed. 'I've only got a permit for two p.m. through four p.m. And don't chase anybody. It's not allowed. There's cameras.'

I count eighteen cameras on buildings and posts.

We sit at the fountain edge. Sheba and Carla chat like they're best friends. I adjust my germ costume and recall some deep questions from my *Philosophy Book*. *Question everything. Notice the absurd. Arrive at large conclusions.* My question is, what is dignity? Can it be preserved while wearing a germ costume? Is the money I am going to earn worth the humiliation I am going to suffer? My big conclusion is that life is a series of disappointments and then you die.

The Square has a tall statue of the Duke of Wellington in the middle of it. Around the statue are stalls with different arty things to do. You can get your name written in Mandarin. Have a go at blowing glass. Pose for a portrait from one of three sketch artists. Join a samba class. The final side of the Square, directly facing the Duke, is a music stage. There's an opera singer doing a solo as we sit.

She's too close to the microphone and I have to hold my ears against the screech. The glass-blower looks nervously at his vases like they might shatter. Someone finds the mic volume control and turns it down just before the whole Square explodes. Phew.

Carla nudges me and hands me leaflets. Sheba's already on her feet. 'Go!' Carla tells us both. 'Love your life! Gobble your germs!'

Me and Sheba jump up and down under the gaze of the Duke. People come over, puzzled at first then smiling at us. One of them asks if she can take a selfie. She's a check-coated, flowery-perfumed, big lady. 'You two have such beautiful smiles,' she says, getting between us and hoisting her selfie stick. It's the first time anyone has ever said that to me in my entire life. I'm usually Leonard the Miserable.

No sooner has she selfied us than someone else asks the same thing. People start queuing. Carla gives us a double-thumbs up. We do about twenty photo sessions before it's lunchtime and we can sit down under the statue. 'Well done, kids,' says Carla. 'You made a lot of people happy and handed out lots of leaflets. Two brilliant germs!'

'It's mega-fun!' says Sheba, sending her amoeba costume rippling with enthusiasm.

Carla nudges me. 'You're allowed to stop smiling now.'

I stop. I feel the soreness in my jaw. Grinning is exhausting.

'I think I'm going to pass out,' Sheba says, tugging at the neckline of her costume to let cold air in.

Carla helps us both get the costumes off. I'm dripping with sweat.

'Would you like me to spend some of your pay on getting you lunch or a drink or something?' Carla says, rubbing Sheba's shoulders to relax her.

Sheba's answer is instant. 'Lunch and drink is included in the meal-deal. It was pay plus lunch. That's what we agreed.'

'Meal deal? I'm not Sainsbury's,' protests Carla.

Sheba won't budge. 'A deal's a deal.'

Carla goes off scowling.

Me and Sheba sit next to each other. A trickle of her sweat rolls on to my arm. She smells sweet still so she must be using deodorant. I wonder how I smell. I glance at her. Her eyes are closed and she's rocking a little to the music from the stage. Her face is the brown of my sister's iPhone case, or that shiny brown you find when you crack open an apple and there's a fresh seed in the middle. With the same smoothness.

'Finished staring?'

How could she see me with her eyes closed?

'You got a bit of fluff on your face,' I say, recovering.

'Take it off then.'

Her eyelashes merge as she closes her eyes and leans her face forward a bit for me. I hesitate, then brush her cheek with my thumb.

'Done.'

'I'll check yours now.' It's a joke but I go along with it. She looks at my face the same way I peered around hers. I close my eyes, waiting for her thumb on my cheek.

'What are you two up to?'

I open my eyes. Sheba's looking guilty as Carla chucks down two tiny bags of crisps and a carton of orange juice each. 'Get that down you fast, your break's over. You've got to hand out another hundred leaflets minimum before 4 p.m.'

She really gets into this being the big boss thing at times, does Carla.

We get back to work. To make things interesting, me and Sheba start doing star jumps and belly bumps in between singing about germs. The samba drummer comes over and lays down a rhythm so we throw in some more moves and before you know it we've got a crowd again. We're becoming famous.

The MC sing-songs into the mic: 'Get over to the fountain to see the Amazing Cheese Strings doing their Samba Sensation!'

The MC calls it Samba because the samba drummer's dancer has got between us and has been showing us moves. The crowd gets bigger and bigger. We're doing spins and cartwheels as well as samba twists. Maybe we get too good because a police officer steps though the crowd and says we're causing an obstruction. He insists on smelling all our breaths to prove we're not drunk because he says they've had reports of rowdy kids intoxicated in the Square.

As he's saying this, a man in a monkey suit starts swinging around the Duke of Wellington's leg, screeching into a loudhailer and throwing key rings in the air that people dash to pick up.

'What about him then?' I ask.

The police officer dismisses me. 'He's allowed. It's Gorilla Awareness Day.'

'Isn't he causing an obstruction though?'

I want to argue more but Carla gets me by the stringy cheese leg stockings and frog-marches me off. People start laughing at us and Carla rolls with it. 'Grab me like that!' cries Sheba, running alongside. Carla obliges. We do this funny dance being hauled off by my sister, who plonks us down on a bench to applause. Life's funny like that, I decide.

As soon as I've sat down, someone wants to shake my hand who I don't recognize.

'Hello, Mrs Podborksy,' says Sheba.

Take away the hat, add a frown, and put behind her some projector slides about erupting volcanoes and yes, it's my Geography teacher. I nod at her, hoping she'll go away fast. The man she's linked arms with, nods at me.

'I was blown away, Leonard and Sarbjit! You two! So much zest and exuberance. Everything you don't show in my lessons!'

I give her my best scowl, but she doesn't take the hint. Instead she does introductions. She pats the man's hand.

'This is Mr Sax, the school Drama teacher. He's looking for recruits, aren't you, Mr Sax? And you two are magnificent!'

Mrs Podborsky's just paid me more compliments in five seconds than she's done in two years at school. Crocodile praise. I'm not fooled.

'Yes, an excellent performance,' Mr Sax says, 'synchronisation, timing …'

Mr Sax can't find the last word he wants. Unlike with Mrs Podborsky, something makes me decide I like him – there's something genuine about him. And even though I'd never in a month of Sundays have anticipated this, I hear myself saying, 'Yeh, I'd give it a go, whatever it is.'

'The Drama Club,' Mr Sax enthuses, then: '"Execution".'

'Execution what, sir?'

'Execution is the word I wanted. You have such immaculate execution. Both of you.'

74

I've got no idea what he means but it sounds good. Sheba's clinging to my arm, saying, 'Isn't it great we've been talent-spotted?' Then she's doing shuffle-dance moves but just with her feet. She broke out into theatrical gasps when Mr Sax piled on the flattery. She's made for theatre.

'Next weekend,' Mr Sax says, ticking two imaginary boxes in the air in front of him, 'I'll be watching for you. You are both Extra. Ord. Inary. Don't let me down!'

Mr Sax and Mrs Podborsky spin away from us into the crowds.

Immediately they're gone, Sheba's rubbing her hands, saying to me, 'Where's your sister? Where's our money?'

I check my phone. It's past 4 p.m. We look around. Mum's turned up and she and Carla are stuffing the two amoeba into Mum's car. We run up. Sheba puts out her hand. 'I believe there's a payment due.'

'Oh, yeh, sorry.'

Carla reaches into her back pocket and pulls out two sealed envelopes. She hands one to Sheba. The other one goes to me.

'Isn't that your sister waving to you over there?' Carla says, pointing by the Duke of Wellington and coaxing Sheba to run off.

Sheba begins opening her envelope.

'Darling, open it later, the money'll blow away,' Carla says.

Sheba opens the envelope. Inside it are two five-pound notes. She rubs the notes together to check.

'This is five pounds short,' Sheba says. 'And his …' she looks at my money … is 'ten pounds short.'

Carla goes stony-faced. 'I've got no more cash on me.'

Sheba keeps her hand out. Her sister is walking towards us.

Mum pipes up. 'Carla, really! Short-changing the poor thing.'

Her sister is two steps away.

Mum gives Sheba a five-pound note. Sheba slips all her money into her trouser pocket. Then she waits, nodding to me and then at Carla and Mum. Reluctantly, Mum unfastens her purse again and gives me a ten-pound note.

'How did it go?' Sheba's sister breezes. She's waving to some bloke with a short moustache and no head hair by the statue as she asks.

'Fun with a double F!' says Sheba. 'Thank you, miss, for the opportunity,' she says to Carla. Then Sheba tugs her sister away.

'You're fired, darling,' Carla mutters after her. Then to Mum, 'Cost me five quid extra, that girl!'

Mum snatches the ten pounds she gave me back out of my hands. 'Fifteen. I can't be giving money away left, right and centre.'

'But Mum …' I protest.

Mum shows me the hand. 'File your complaint with Carla!'

And I reflect there's truth in the saying of the Ancient Egyptians (if I remember it rightly): *What is given with one hand is most often taken back double quick with the other.*

A sign proclaims proudly that we are in the waiting room of *Nynonis Jors, Hypnotist to the Stars*. I consider that real stars – the stuff up in the sky – must be one of the few things beyond the influence of hypnotists, but I let this thought slide.

The waiting room is the only place I've sat in, in all my life, that has mirrors on its ceiling. The mirrors are not straight reflecting mirrors, they seem to bend the light, like fairground mirrors, so everyone in the waiting room with us has these strange proportions. For instance, the little old lady holding the fluffy dog has arms as burly as a wrestler's yet her dog looks as slim as a squeegee. Meanwhile, the man in the corner with the baseball cap on back to front has a forehead that stretches for miles and then a tiny rose of a mouth.

Mum nudges me to stop staring at the ceiling so I look down. *Notice the small things.* At shoes.

The shoes directly opposite me are weather-beaten white tennis pumps. Emerging from the collar of these pumps at the back is a grey woolly sock with grey-black bobbles, then a little above are the edges of grey nylon, turned-up trousers. Then a light salmon, Fred Perry T-shirt shows off Popeye forearms, bulging biceps and shoulders so big they have swallowed up the person's neck. I try to guess why he's calling at the hypnotists. Body-builder tablets addiction?

Next along are some shoes in the shiniest red imaginable. The front of the shoe is shaped like two red tongues that cross over before lashing together at the back. Red toenails peep out of the front and a long black dagger stem with a glinting steel cap at its floor end make the high heel of the shoe. The shoes enclose smooth feet that rise into sleek calves which slide up to dimpled knees which are wrapped one over the other. A snug red skirt envelops the thighs, which probably belong on a catwalk.

I try to guess why the wearer of the red shoes has come and decide she must be here to cure her shyness, because appearances can be deceptive.

In the space between the waiting-room door and consultation door, two black, bulbously round shoes house feet in silver socks that are met by matt black trousers which have a line of silk running along their sides from hem to waist of a shininess that would have had our Carla gasping (but she's not here because Mum dropped her off at the bus stop). The black shoes and showbiz pants zig and zag and swish and swash and tap and tip up and down the aisle in almost a hopscotch pattern but sometimes moving backwards or forwards as if the feet are suddenly afraid of certain floorboards. Nobody bats an eyelid as this strange behaviour takes place. I guess addiction to dance or to gambling.

Mum nudges me again, this time to look up. There's no pleasing some folk. A woman in a pink fur coat around her neck comes out of the Consultation Room and crosses the waiting room with a smile on her face so blissful, her feet hardly touch the ground.

'Mrs Blackwood?'

The caller is wearing black cowboy boots, high-waist black trousers and a yellow shirt that has its upper three buttons open to reveal a red and gold medallion with the word *YES* in the middle. His mousy brown hair is done in a choirboy haircut and he has very large, very white teeth.

We go in. The room is painted pea-green and has a tiled white floor that makes your shoes click and tap as you walk to the seats. His desk is of transparent glass and has nothing at all on it.

'Come in, sit down. Just checking, who are you here to see?'

'The hypnotist,' Mum snaps. She's a bit vexed at the wait she's endured. Almost an hour.

'There are several of us. Which one?'

Mum gets a card out of her purse and reads it. 'Mr Nynonis Jors?'

'Excellent. That's me. Let's just get the pronunciation right though.'

'Did I say it wrong?'

'Not your fault. Can you say it again, but the first name, where you see the first two N's, they are actually pronounced as an M. Try again.'

'Mr Mymonis Jors.'

'Very good. And now the J in the last name, is pronounced as a Y. Have a go.'

'Yors?' tries Mum, straight away.

'Good, good. Now put it all together.'

'Mr Mymonis Yors.'

'And again.'

'Mr Mymonis Yors.'

'Once more.'

'Mr Mymonis Yors!' Mum shouts at him.

'Excellent. How can I help? Let's get to it. Big queue waiting outside.'

On the wall behind the hypnotist hangs one of those plug-in pictures of the sea that has a 3D effect so the waves in it look like they're actually moving. The rest of the wall holds certificates, an eyesight test-type chart, and a mini-grandfather clock.

'I want to stop smoking and he wants to remove his zombie obsession. We're here for the two-for-one deal.

Here is the coupon.' Mum takes out a coupon she must have clipped from the local newspaper they shove through our door every Thursday.

'Ah.' The hypnotist takes the coupon from her and looks at it. 'That ran out. It says on it, "Ends Saturday".'

'This is Saturday.'

'Yes, it ended at the first second after midnight Friday. As soon as Saturday started, it ended.'

Mum's not having it. 'It's still Saturday. It ends at the end of office hours, Saturday.'

The hypnotist lowers his head and leans forward a little in his chair so the medallion pops out of his shirt. 'I'll not argue with you, Mrs Blackwood. I don't have time. Have you got the money? It's eighty pounds.'

Mum fishes her purse from her bag, unfolds four twenty-pound notes and hands them over to him.

'OK, I'll do you the smoking and, if I've got time, I'll see about him and his zombies – but there's no guarantee.' He screws up the token Mum handed him and throws it in a bin under the desk.

A series of grumbling sounds come out of Mum's mouth but nothing that is an actual word.

'I understand,' Mr Jors says. 'You had a hard and boring day today, didn't you?'

'Yes,' says Mum.

'Keep looking at me. You've had a very busy day, right?'

'Yes.'

'Your eyes are tired. What are they?'

'Tired.'

'They're closing, aren't they?'

'Yes.' Mum closes her eyes.

Mr Jors holds each of the twenty-pound notes up to the light then, satisfied, pops them in his back trouser pocket.

'OK, listen to me, Mrs Blackwood, you're hypnotized. What are you?'

'Hypnotized.'

'And you no longer like smoking. What did I say?'

'You no longer like smoking.'

'And again. "I no longer like smoking." Repeat that.'

'I no longer like smoking.'

'It reminds me of rotting fish.'

'It reminds me of rotting fish.'

'Excellent. Now I'm going to count backwards from ten and when I reach one, you're going to be wide awake and back in the room. Ten, nine, eight … seven, six, five … four, three … two, one.'

Mum opens her eyes. She starts talking immediately. 'There, you've got my money. When are you going to hypnotize me?'

'I already did.'

'No, you didn't.'

'Look, I did. I've got your money and you no longer like smoking.'

'Baloney, you've done nothing.'

'Ask him.'

Mum looks across at me. She looks slightly cross-eyed and very confused. I tell her gently: 'He hypnotized you, Mum.'

Mum's in her fight-everyone mood. She turns back to Mr Jors.

'You mean you let him watch?'

'You wanted a two for one, so I did him at the same time. He no longer likes smoking either.'

'He's never smoked!'

'That's what you think.' Mr Jors turns to me. Mum turns to me.

'Look at the medallion, young man. Three, two, one, you're under. Have you ever smoked?'

I hear myself saying as if from far away: 'Now and then.'

'Three, two, one, you're back in the room.'

'See?'

'But I want him cured of zombies, not smoking.'

'You still want him to smoke?'

'Stop twisting things. Just stop his zombie obsession.' Mum's almost in tears now.

'I'll give him a first session but zombies aren't easy; he'd have to come again.'

'Listen, you'll get no more money out of me. Now remove his zombies!'

Mr Jors sighs and looks at his watch. He realizes what I realized many years ago. There is no point arguing with my mum once she's made up her mind about something.

'OK, just this once,' he concedes.

He turns to me. 'Now Leonard,' he says, angling his chair so he's looking directly at me. 'You've had a long day, haven't you?'

'Yes.'

'Lots of chasing around?'

'Yes.'

'Lots of earache from your mum?'

'Yes.'

'You're profoundly tired. What are you?'

'Profoundly tired.'

'When I count down from three you're going to be under but you will keep your eyes open. Understand?'

'Yes.'

'Three, two … one, you're under. Look at the water feature on the wall there. You saw it before and you liked it, didn't you?'

'Yes.'

'Now I want you to bring the zombies into your mind … slowly, all of them … all right. Are they all there?'

'Yes.'

'Where have they come from?'

'My house and the park.'

'Bring them all together into this room … OK, now you see the water feature? It's become a raging, freezing cold sea.'

'OK.'

'And I want you to watch the zombies. You seeing them still?'

'Yes.'

'They don't like water but watch them. They're walking into that deep, raging sea. And they sink all the way to the bottom of that sea. And disappear. The zombies are no more, they've dissolved like salt dissolves in the ocean. Are there any more zombies?'

'There are no more zombies.'

'Say it again.'

'No more zombies.'

'Good. Now I'm going to count backwards from seven and on the count of one you'll come back into the room. Seven, six … five, four, three … two … one. And you're back in the room.'

'Mum, I'm starving, can we go now?'

'What do you mean I gave you an ear-bashing?'

'What are you talking about, Mum?'

The hypnotist coughs loudly. 'Your smoking is gone for ever, Mrs Blackwood, and the zombies will not be back any time soon but as I say, it's a difficult one, zombies. If you're prepared to pay for a thirty-pounds booster, I can guarantee no more zombies.'

Mum's off her seat. 'Not a penny more, you'll get off me, Mr NyNonis Jors.'

He smiles. 'Now one more look into the medallion, both of you ... You've just had a wonderful neck and foot massage. You're both feeling blissed as a parrot in sunshine.'

Then Mr Yors is standing over us, tapping his watch. 'You have to leave now.'

I check his medallion. It says HAPPY in the middle of it.

Mum stands and offers her hand. 'Thank you for the hypnotism. I feel quite refreshed, Mr Nynonis Jors.'

'Excellent,' says Mr Jors. He opens the consultation-room door for us. Mum floats all the way out to the car.

We get home and the electrics have been fixed so at least we've got light. Mum spends the rest of the evening with a bucket of bleach because she says everywhere smells of rotting fish. I go to bed and don't see any zombies for the whole night.

THE THEATRE OF TEARS

Our school gym needs a health warning. When you step in, your nose immediately freaks. Years of ponging socks and stinky underwear has sunk into every crack and crevice, every brick, every rope and every piece of creaking equipment. The stink pole-axes your nose. And yet within seconds, you stop smelling it. Instead, the reek of ancient school dinners rises up from the canteen. In moments, that vanishes too. The nose has a brilliant Memory Delete button.

Me, Eddie and Sheba have burst through the doors for Saturday Drama Club. We're late because Eddie took ages to gel his hair. We gag at the smell in here but walk into the centre of the room, where twelve kids are sitting while Mr Sax looms over them, throwing blue and yellow cards in their laps.

'In pairs, please. If you have tears, let me see you shed them. If joy, let me see it unbound. Go, thespians!'

The Drama Club kids scatter, leaving us standing in front of Mr Sax.

'So glad you could make it,' he says. 'It's Sheba, Leonard and …?'

'Eddie,' I say. 'He wanted to come too.'

'I can dance,' Eddie says. He breaks into a shuffle.

Mr Sax nods with approval as Eddie does his thing. Finally, he says, 'You're a regular marvel, Eddie. Audition over. Drama Club membership application is approved.'

Eddie does a little bow. Mr Sax fans out a set of cards in each hand for us to choose one card from each hand.

'Have a go at the exercise,' he tells us. 'You have to read the blue card, which is either a weather report or instructions for an appliance – using the emotion of the yellow card.'

I've got joy and how to fold an ironing board. Sheba has sorrow and a forecast of snow. Eddie has in-love and opening a can of beans. Eddie goes first. He's gross and hilarious.

I try a little dance with the ironing board as I read out the *place this here while holding that there*-type instructions. I have the imaginary ironing board collapse on me. Sheba and Eddie pretend to pull me out of it.

Sheba does no dance or movement for her weather forecast. She simply sits cross-legged, lifts puppy eyes and slowly but steadily says, "Today … will be … snow. On the word 'snow', tears well up in her eyes.

We were late to start so most people have finished their exercise and are gathered round us. Sheba's tears continue to spill as she keeps going.

'Snow … on the hills … and snow … on the ground.'

We're all quiet. Those are real tears spilling down her cheeks.

Mr Sax breaks the spell. 'What a great performance, give her a clap!' he calls out. 'Now, stars, you must all twinkle in our next exercise …'

I'm learning that you hardly ever catch your breath at Drama Club. Mr Sax whips us into re-enacting The Siege of Rome. In groups of three, two people play the chariot and a third person clambers on them and is carried round waving an imaginary sword, slaying gladiators and peasants who stand in the middle of the gym in a huddle. That segues into a 'funny walk' contest. Then we do Talking Hands. Person One speaks, Person Two lip-synches the speech and Person Three stands behind Person Two and acts as their arms.

I start and Eddie lip-synches me describing how to give a dog a bath and Sheba is Eddie's hands, doing all the shampooing. Then Eddie talks for Sheba as Sheba flies a runaway plane and I'm her hands. The best bit is where I have to wipe the sweat off Sheba's brow then cover her eyes as the plane swoops low and just misses the watchtower. We run out of time at that point. We have to find three new partners and do a trust game.

'Put your feet together, fold your arms across your chest, close your eyes and let yourself fall backwards. The other three people in your group catch you. Show them, Roxy.' On cue, Roxy does a perfect flop and her group catch her.

'This time,' announces Mr Sax, 'we're doing it without mats. You know each other much better now. Trust yourselves. Trust each other.'

The three in my new group don't look fit for purpose. Vona is wearing an eye-patch after poking her own eye last week and, based on how she kept letting the rubber mat slip as we pulled it off the gym floor into the storage room, has very dodgy eye-hand coordination. Seamus is a human fly. He lands on some thought. He stays on it.

But at random moments, he gets up and wanders off. And the lanky boy whose name I don't know goes into these two-second trances when you're talking to him when he hears nothing and notices nothing.

We start off by falling a little way with a plan to gradually fall further. First time round, the lanky boy forgets to catch me and Seamus lets me fall too far. Second time round, Vona catches me but lets me slip and it's only because of the lanky boy that I don't crash to the floor. I'm about to say I'm not going to do it any more when out of nowhere, Sheba barges in and begs to join our group.

'You're not allowed!' the others say but we stand our ground till they give in. We do the exercise as a group of five. It feels safer with Sheba. Sheba goes last and when it's her turn, she makes me swear I'll catch her.

'No fooling?' she tests.

'On my mum's life.'

'If you drop me I'll never speak to you again.'

'Shut up and close your eyes.'

'What?'

'C'mon, Sheebs, trust me.'

The tears well up in her again, real ones. The others groan, thinking it's another charade. I put an arm around her. She sniffles into my sleeve.

'What's wrong? It's only an exercise. Remember what Mr Sax said, you have the right to not do stuff you don't like.'

She looks up at me. She's stopped crying. 'Maybe I need to do it … You've got to catch me though.'

'Course.'

She wipes her eyes, fixes on a smile and we step back into the group. The lanky boy and Seamus stop play-

88

fighting and Vona stops trying to touch her nose with her tongue. We take our positions behind Sheba, who crosses her arms and calls out 'Ready?' Somehow, without saying anything, everyone understands we've got to get it right for her.

And we do. We catch her.

Drama Club finishes with a group hug and then me and Sheeba wait while Eddie spends a year in the bathroom gelling his hair again. He's got an obsession with it. He comes out with a puffed-up quiff and spraying half a can of deodorant on himself.

The sun's out but somehow it also starts raining. Eddie and Sheba leap under a tree but I keep walking. Dollops of it drum on my head, ping off my jacket, splatter into my trousers, bounce off my schoolbag. I can see a bus shelter ahead. It's two-tone. There's this band of black–clothed bodies in the shelter and then the smaller upper band of white for the faces. The people peer out from the shelter the way herded sheep do, heads pointing in the same direction. As I approach, the sheep all turn to me. They stiffen. Sheba sprints past me and dives into the shelter.

I reach the shelter space. It's still chucking it down but the people under the shelter have become a solid block and I can't find a gap to get in. Sheba appears between two adults' shoulders. 'Rush in!' she says, then to everyone and no one: 'Give him room!'

Nobody budges. Suddenly Eddie comes running up behind me. He rockets himself in. Sheba gives him a high five. 'Way to go, Eddie!'

Eddie calls to me from the shelter. 'Come on. Lenny, run in!'

I walk back five steps, take a run and leap like Eddie.

People put their hands out and I'm pushed back out.

'What is wrong with you all?' Eddie shouts at them.

Eddie and Sheba grab me between them and haul me in. There's lots of complaints. We ignore them. There's enough room if people shuffled up. We stand there, facing out.

And I think to myself: It rains on everyone – robbers and judges, zombies and humans. But why does it always rain on me just that little bit more than it rains on anyone else? As if listening, the rain suddenly stops. The bus-shelter crowd expands, spilling out on to the pavement and flowing away as fast as the water rushing into the gutter at our feet.

Eddie takes off. Me and Sheba wait for the bus. I wonder why she was crying – twice – but I can't think how to ask her. Eventually I find something.

'Were those tears real, Sheba?'

'I don't know.'

I consider that for a moment. 'How did you do it?'

'I didn't.'

Now I'm confused. We both stand there. I see Sheba puzzling out her own thoughts and feelings.

'Maybe it was because Nana was losing her mind this morning and everyone was upset. She was bawling about she can't find a needle and she has to feed the goats and isn't the moon-landing today. Stuff like that. We can't trust her on her own any more.'

'OK.'

'And then sometimes at a certain time of the month I can cry easily anyway, but you wouldn't understand about that – it's a girl thing.'

I think I understood a little, what with living with two females. But I keep quiet.

'Or maybe I cry when I'm happy and I was happy doing drama – I liked it.'

'True. It's fun.'

I'm holding her hand. I don't know how that happened. Sheba takes her hand from mine and brushes tears from her eyes with it.

PART 2

ELECTRIC CHICKEN

Mr Sax says he needs us to do rehearsals every Saturday. I tell The Windmill and he says I shouldn't give up on the football now, not when I'm showing promise and I'm helping the whole team. I tell him I want to try drama.

'If your football's a hobby, fine,' says The Windmill. 'But with you, Lenny, it's more than that, isn't it? It's a passion. Something's changed in you, Leonard, and I can't figure out what it is.'

'I've started to smile more, sir,' I say.

'Then I want the old, miserable Leonard back!'

We both laugh at that. He's all right, is The Windmill.

A few Saturdays later, and I find I miss the football. Jamal has started podcasting his match commentaries on SoundCloud. It's not the same as being on the touchline, but I tune into them when I can. He mostly makes me feel sad for the team.

Jamal's Podcast
Juicy Ducie footballers are making the ball dance nicely. There goes Marcus on a run. Marcus passes to Horse. And Horse has booted it into the sky. Our forwards go running after. And get it. They're chasing towards the goal. Will

we score? It's close, we're through. It's impossible not to. It's ... we've missed! How could we miss? The ball is 6 centimetres – I'm telling you *6 centimetres* – from the goal line. To miss? It defies all the laws of physics. All the laws of trigonometry, geometry, algebra and all the others they teach us in maths. It's a whopping miss. I wouldn't like to be in Kwong's shoes now.

Our heads have dropped. The ball is zoomed up to the other end and ... it's in the back of our net. That makes it 12:0. We're losing *12 nil*. Is there a planet anywhere where people play more rubbish than this? I don't think so. This football match has fizzled. 12 nil. It can't get any worse than this. Oh no. I take that back. It can. It has. They've scored again. From a corner. That's 13 nil. This is beyond despair. This is beyond hope. The worries of the world are woven on the team's faces as they trudge back to the semi-circle for the restart. It's the day the earth collapsed. The calamity that no number of protein shakes can cure. The final whistle blows. And I am speechless with tears. That's me, Jamal, on Podcast 873.5. Check my Twitter. Check my Insta. Check my everything. I'm speechless. It's been a massacre. Jamal, speechless, signing off.

I try to put it out of my mind and I keep going to drama. Four Saturdays later and we're starting work on a musical. Mr Sax says he might cast me and Sheba as the lead characters because we can sing and dance and he knows we're not afraid of massive crowds, which is what Mr Sax promises we'll have on Opening Night.

There are about twenty of us in Drama Club, aged eleven to fourteen. We do physical exercises and voice warm-ups, then practise acting techniques in small groups under the guidance of our maestro.

Mr Gordon Horatio Sax has big hair, large breasts, strong thighs, a feathery scarf, moleskin blue trousers, purple glasses and a black polo-neck jumper. He also has a booming voice thanks to his Royal Academy of Dramatic Art training, where he nearly shared a dressing room with Benedict Cumberbatch. He speaks in such a way that ev-er-y syl-a-ble is pro-per-ly ar-tic-u-la-ted. He's an ace theatre director who gets the best out of people using a variety of techniques including:

Imploring: in which he bends on one knee and tugs your sleeve while widening his eyes and sucking in his cheeks in an orphaned-boy-pleading manner.

Flouncing: in which he waves his arms in the air as if he's being attacked by imaginary bees while rushing from one imaginary post to another.

Praising to the heavens: in which the phrases 'this child is a genius'; 'destined for greatness'; and 'I will treasure this moment for the rest of my life' occur repeatedly.

Tearing out his hair: in which he sinks to his knees, claws his cheeks, slides his fingers over his ears to the back of his head then grasps his hair with both hands, bawls and calls for someone to 'go find my mummy!'.

And getting everyone to do group hugs: in which all the actors have to come together in an ever-decreasing circle until everyone is crushed up against each other, then we lock arms while he intones, 'There is so much love in the room, so much talent in this room, so, let me SEE IT!' Then we have to break and redo the scene that we've messed up but this time ten times BETTER!

If we had Mr Sax for every lesson and not just Drama Club we'd all come out with 'A' stars in everything. I told him this and he went red, said, 'It's not true but you've made my day.' Then he took his hankie out of his back pocket and wiped his eyes.

We're in groups devising and Mr Sax goes round listening in to the sketches we develop, giving us tips and encouraging us. At last he calls us all to attention.

'Group One, you were given *Swan Lake* as your idea. What have your fabulous minds generated? Remember, everyone, this is a creative session – so no booing, no jeers, only clapping. Every idea is a beautiful idea. Group One, will your tribune please stand up.'

'Sir, we've come up with *Murder at the Secret Lake*,' says the rust-haired tribune of Group One, standing up.

'Pray tell me more.'

'These two wild swans get attacked at the Secret Lake and the fishermen go mad because they loved the swans and they murder the people that did it and dump their bodies in the lake. Only, the bodies come back up because of decomposition gas and that, and they come alive as the living dead and kill the fishermen.'

There is silence. Everyone's trying not to laugh.

'Excellent,' says Mr Sax finally. 'You got a lake in and you got swans in. Pat yourselves on the back for that. A lake brimming with dead bodies. We'll find the musical in that if we have to.'

He turns to the next group which has me, Sheba and Eddie in it.

'Ah the shining stars of Group Two, astonish me with your brilliance. You were given *Romeo and Juliet: The Musical*. How fared you? Proffer forth thy tribune.'

Eddie stands up. 'We've got *Death in the Boar's Head Canal*,' he says.

'Another resounding, musical-like title. Expand. Enlarge. Sweeten my ears with an elaboration.'

'Sir, this Asian girl falls in love with this white boy only she's not allowed to because her family want her to marry someone else. The boy has the hots for her …'

'Pray, what are "the hots"?'

'In love. He's really in love with her, sir. But they're miserable because even if the girl's family allow them to see each other, his family don't like Asians and his brother says they'll kill him if he goes out with her. Things get worse and worse …'

'No doubt. How does this happy romance end?'

'They share a last pizza then she jumps into the canal to kill herself. He jumps in after her, though nobody knows if it was to kill himself or to rescue her. To add mystery, sir.'

'That's the ending?'

'Yes, sir, they both die. Based on a true story, sir – it was in the papers.'

'A tragic tale of woe for the song, dance and shimmering splendidness of the musical genre to drape itself upon. Children, is your world this bleak? Is there no hope?'

'There wasn't none in *Romeo and Juliet* either, sir. I think,' Eddie replies.

'So true, so true. Star-crossed lovers. Let us move on to our final group, Group Three. Your prompt was *Razzmatazz: The Musical!*. Will your story involve troubling the local undertakers too? Tribune of Group Three, what say you?'

A girl with a row of school badges on her jacket stands up.

'Our story is *Love on the Roller Rink*.'

'No deaths?'

'None whatsoever, sir.'

'What-so-ever?'

'No, sir.'

'Lord, kiss me on the lips! Carry on, child.'

'There's these two groups of skateboarders and they go to the skateboard park every week. The two groups meet and make friends because they find they like each other and they have a really nice time.'

'Is that it?'

'Yes.'

'I smell genius in that idea. Movement. Flow. Happiness. And no corpses.'

He turns again. 'Now, it's time for your improvisation exercises. Get into groups of four and stretch your bodies from fingers to toes and imagine …'

There's a wallop at the back of the hall and the fire doors clang open. In steps The Windmill, followed by seven footballers in full football kit including boots with studs in – a breach of the gym rules. They put their hands on their hips and look around like they could beat us up if they decided they wanted to.

Mr Sax spins round and holds out a big STOP hand.

'Mr Brod-er-rick, what is the meaning of this intrusion?'

'I come in peace,' Mr Windmill replies, as he leads his players into the centre of the hall like the Roman invasion. 'You will remember the agreement we made last fortnight, Mr Sax?'

'An agreement was made? Between ourselves?' Mr Sax makes it sound absurd, as if he is a Roman Emperor and The Windmill a lowly peasant. This throws The Windmill.

'Well, yes, we had a conversation in the staff room. By the coffee machine.'

'Ah, that coffee machine. The coffee it dispenses – many have experienced hallucinations after drinking it. What visions did you have?'

'That you were going to teach our football team how to dive properly.'

'I agreed to teach your army of urchins how to cheat effectively in the game of soccer?'

'That was the agreement. It's not cheating, it's part of the game now. Theatrics. "Expressionism", I think you called it.'

'Perhaps the conversation occurred with the Fine Art teacher, "Expressionism" being a word more used in that school of thought than in drama?'

'No, it was you. I recall perfectly – I made a note. And you said to come today. So here we are. We discussed it. What we want to learn is the Italian Roll, the German Dive-Bomb, and the Argentinean Plank.'

Mr Sax thinks a moment. 'Well, all right, Mr Brod-er-rick. I have a vague recollection of some such conversation with you. But we have no need for any nationalist stereotyping. If we have to conduct this exercise, then my thespian geniuses will devise routines which will be uniquely brilliant.'

Like all of us, The Windmill hasn't understood a word of what Mr Sax said. 'Does that mean you'll help, then?' he replies.

'In the school of theatre, it comes under "fight scenes". Very useful skill, along with duelling. Yes. Just for you, you charmer, Mr Brod-er-rick, we shall give it a go.'

'Thank you, Mr Sax, thank you very much. You don't know how much the team needs you and your expertise.'

'Hold the flattery for now, Mr Brod–er–rick. Judge me by results. Footballers – take off thy metal-clad boots!'

Mr Sax has us clear the floor, drag out the rubber mats and stand in a circle.

'Is this really happening?' I ask Sheba.

She laughs. 'Diving lessons! Yeah! I love it!'

Once all the mats are in place and the groups are sorted out, Mr Sax begins the diving lesson.

'Thespians, partner up, two or three of you to a footballer. Don't worry, they won't bite. We're going to learn the art of falling and its three component parts. The Anticipation. The Act Proper. And the Aftermath. Everyone shake their hands in the air, now shake your legs, wiggle your hips, let's get ready for a superb, sporting performance.'

We're soon warmed up. Mr Sax begins.

'First comes Anticipation. The merest brush. The smallest nudge. And you are horrified. Look at each other in pairs. Horrified. Jaws drop, eyes pop, tongues out, neck stiff. You are seized with the anticipation of mortal pain.'

He demonstrates and then gives us three minutes to rehearse. We all practise our shock-horror faces as Mr Sax wanders round giving us tips until he's happy.

'Excellent. Now the Act Proper. At the point of actual contact, you have stumbled into an electric fence and cannot get yourself off it. Let's see that. Show those thousand volts surging through your bodies. Stagger. Bend your knees.'

Mr Sax demonstrates. 'At the same time shake your arms like a four year old frantically trying to shake money out of his brother's piggy bank before his brother gets back. Face, eyes, cheeks, eyebrows, should be all a-quiver. Let's see it!'

The entire hall resounds to the shake of electrified bodies.

'Marvellous!' The Windmill shouts above the din, genuinely pleased with proceedings. He starts going round looking, encouraging: 'Didn't I say you needed more shake when you went down, Marcus? Fabulous. Horse – the cheeks, more wobble, more horror in the eyes, please. Yakub, your knees are frozen. Knees of an electrified chicken, please.'

It's nice to see The Windmill like this. Most times we see him he's so miserable about us losing and his enthusiasm is fake. But here, he's more real.

Mr Sax's voice booms out. 'Now the Aftermath. It is not enough to fall down. You must imagine you have been hit by the high-velocity bullet of an ace sniper. Watch and learn …'

Mr Sax suddenly crumples, his hand holding his heart. He slams into the floor and his limbs go inert, star-shaped. He gets up. 'Have you got that? Bullet. Heart. Clutch. On your face is the realization this is your final breath on earth. Then fall dead. Not a twitch. Like a fish on ice. Go to it, dear thespians: *dulce et decorum est pro Ducie High mori!*'

'What's that mean, sir?' someone shouts out. He's showing off his Latin and we know it.

'Sweet and noble it is to die for your school team. It shall be stitched into all the Football Coaching badges one day, no doubt. Very well – get dying, everyone. Die gloriously and repeatedly. Happy, Mr Brod-er-rick?'

'Yes, very happy,' says The Windmill. He's ecstatic. He shouts, 'Horse, if only you could die every Saturday like that, we wouldn't be buried at the bottom of the League!'

Mr Sax continues the lesson over the noise. 'Extremities, please! What have I told you? I want to see poetry in the hand shapes, the legs properly articulated, hips rocked forward at the sudden shock. Come on, let's not get lazy, let's die great deaths!'

After twenty-five minutes of sniper-shot dying, we move on to face-palm mimes.

'Someone pushes you in the face. Place a hand towards your face. Suddenly look as if you have run into thick plate-glass. Footballers, stand and watch the professionals who have done this already when we did mime. Let me hear those groans, class. Good flow of the hand, articulation of the elbows, and the shoulders rock nicely. Most important is the head – press sideways into the glass, lips apart, brow anguished. Now catapult yourself on to the floor. Excellent catapult, Yassy, but you forgot the face-squish first, so try again. Let's do this right. Concentrate, darlings!'

I'm paired off with Josh. He's a defender and rubbish because he's not fast enough on his feet. I try to coach him but his heart's not in it.

'This is daft,' he says. 'My game's staying on my feet, not falling over. It's only strikers want to fall over.'

I have sympathy for him. 'It's only a bit of fun. Have a go,' I tell him.

He does quite a good belly flop after my pep talk. Mr Sax notices.

'That's it, help each other,' he calls out. That's another thing I like about him, he notices when you do something extra.

'Thespians, use your mirror technique so the footballers can see how they're doing. Five more minutes!'

All around me people are flopping, shivering, rolling, bug-eyeing, groaning, writhing, agonizing and swanning to the floor. It's like a zombie convention.

'OK, let's calm down a little bit. This requires our brains.' Mr Sax gets us to sit down in a circle as he explains what Recovery is. His voice drops into a theatrical whisper that can still be heard as far as the fire door. 'You hear the whistle. You've won your free kick. Thespians, what happens when you don't have a line but you're still on stage? What do you do?'

'Stay in character!' all us actors shout out in unison.

'Very good. Stay. In. Character. You do not leap up at the sound of the whistle. Or give a thumbs-up sign to your teammates. Or tip a wink to one of your friends on the touchline. Or stick your tongue out at the player who tackled you. Otherwise you may get booked yourself. Is that correct, Mr …?'

'Correct,' The Windmill interrupts before Mr Sax can murder his name again.

'Stay in character,' Mr Sax stage-whispers again, 'stay injured. Everybody up again, limp up, touch the ground like a tender toddler, hold your hip, wince a little. Hobble to the ball. Await perhaps the coach's magic spray.'

'Sponge actually,' The Windmill chips in. 'We can't afford sprays.'

'Fine. Give it at least ten seconds before you completely recover. Allow the cold water from that sponge to sink in, OK, let's see that for the final five minutes. It's free-style time. No partners, just walk around, in pain, limping. Let's see who wins "Best Injured Player Performance Award".'

We do limping for two minutes then we gather in a circle, and anyone who wants can perform their Aftermath routine, or any other. The footballers perform OK, but everyone agrees that the Drama Club crew nail it. We do a group hug. The footballers look sad: yet again they've lost. I feel sorry for them. This whole thing is a new low in the history of our school football team.

I sit down on the gym floor and pull my shoes back on. The kitchen smells aren't coming through so strongly at the moment. There's only a bit of stale shoe odour and a hint of rubber from the mats we've hauled off the floor and stacked up at the end of the session. I quite like the rubber smell. You can see the tiny specks of black on the gym floor where grains of tired old rubber have broken off.

Eddie jumps down next to me and messes my hair, which is what he does sometimes when he's happy. 'I came second in Electrocution!' he boasts. He bounces up and showcases his electrocution moves. When all of Eddie wobbles and he does his eye-flips at the same time, there's no way you can keep a straight face. Sheba slaps him on the back.

The Windmill and Mr Sax both come over to us.

'Leonard, I have nothing but respect for the efforts of Mr Brod-er-rick in trying to knock together a decent football team.'

'Right, sir,' I say, standing up and trying to figure where the conversation is heading. Eddie and Sheba are on either side of me.

'You were showing amazing promise,' The Windmill tells me. 'Helping with training, throw-in tactics, penalties – all three of you were coming along fantastically.'

'Thank you, sir,' says Eddie.

I get a text. I sneak a look. It's from my mum. The usual.

Never mind darling, you'll win next time maybe xxxxMumxxxx

I put my phone back in my pocket and smile, thinking of my mum feeling sorry for me. She doesn't yet know I've switched to drama. I'll tell her soon.

Mr Sax cuts to the quick. 'I had no idea when I invited you to join the Drama Club that I would be ripping the promising heart out of Mr Broderick's team.'

The Windmill shuffles and sniffs, as if Mr Sax's words have moved him. 'True, true,' he says.

'That said, you Leonard, and Sheba, and Eddie, you show incredible – in-cred-ible – talent as treaders of the boards.'

'That mean actors, sir?' asks Sheba.

'Indeed it does.'

Sheba high-fives Eddie, who does a little shuffle move.

Mr Sax continues: 'So it looks as if you three are faced with a difficult choice. Acting or football. Which is it to be?'

'Acting, sir,' Sheba says straight away.

'Acting, sir,' Eddie chimes.

'And you, Leonard?' asks The Windmill directly. His eyes are brimful of pleading.

'I'm, I'm … I'll think about it, sir.'

'Good,' says Mr Sax. 'A star of the glittery stage or a master of the muddy field. Difficult choice but one only you can make. Let us know before next Saturday which you choose.'

'I will, sir,' I say, nodding to both teachers.

The two of them walk away. I glance at The Windmill. His hands are chopping the air in front of him as he talks to Mr Sax, the way he chops air when he talks about why our tactics didn't work when we lose. He looks unbearably sad. Mr Sax puts his arm round him. They talk some more.

Drama Club's over for the day and me and Sheba are walking home. My body feels loose from all the stretching exercises. Even my face feels looser. Maybe that's why I smile more, I think: my smile muscles get stretched as part of the face exercises.

'Who are you pulling faces at?' asks Sheba, mirroring me.

'He's great, Mr Sax, isn't he?' I reply, setting my face straight.

'I love him,' says Sheba. She kicks up a pop can then volleys it away.

'You're ab-so-lute-ly certain you're doing theatre over football?' I ask her.

'Hell, yeh. So long as I can persuade my fam.'

I stretch my arms. 'What's that mean?'

'My grandma might say, *Teri beti toh vaisya ban rai hai!*'

'Huh?' I know it's bad, but I don't know what she said.

'Actors in our culture, in Grandma's time, were entertainment for men. You know – like whores. That's why we're not supposed to get involved in plays and acting and stuff. Gives you a bad reputation.'

It takes my head a few moments to understand this. 'But didn't your mum let you do the street theatre thing with me?'

'No. That was my sister that spoke to your Carla, not my mum.'

'Your sister approves?'

'I blackmail her to keep her gob shut.'

It's too complicated for me. 'What?'

Sheba lays it out. 'My sister has a boyfriend who she's not meant to have. Geddit? So I tell her, unless she does my wishes, "I'll spill the beans on your boyfriend to Mum! *Tera romeo ki baat Ma se karu!*"

I like the way her whole body changes when she speaks her other language.

I consider Sheba's family manoeuvres in all their chess-like glory and tell her my conclusion. 'You are as smart as a Rubik's Cube, Sheebs.'

Sheba preens. 'I'm not top at maths for nothing!' She draws closer to me. 'I'm dreading telling Mum though. She thinks I'm doing flower-arranging. I'll have to make a Duke of Edinburgh Flower Certificate to show her.'

'Like we can't fake one from the millions of those Certificates on the internet already?'

She laughs and I can see she likes the idea. The wind whips up a bit. I go to put my arm in hers just as she goes to put her arm in mine. We tangle.

'What are we doing?'

'It's cold.'

'Yeah. We can link arms but we can't hold hands.'

I give her a *why*? look.

'Linking arms is friendship. Holding hands is boyfriend zone.'

'I'm down with that.'

We walk along, arms linked until her turn-off point.

'Sabbi, whatever you decide I'm cool with it.'

'Yeh, and whatever you decide, I'm cool with it!' she replies.

I walk away thinking Sheba's a wicked liar and why do I already miss her when she's only been gone two seconds? I reflect, This is how life is. Nothing good ever lasts long.

That night I listen to Jamal's podcast of the latest match the football team's played.

Jamal's Podcast

We are here in the Land of Giants. The other team are a metre higher than our players. We've let in six goals already even though our goalie has been amazing. A fierce wind is blowing. It picks the ball up and drops it at Horse's feet. Horse knocks it forward. Marcus zings up the wing and crosses it high. The wind has suddenly changed direction. The ball's fizzling in the air. One of their giant players heads it. Up it goes again into our goal area. Our goalie's got it covered. But no, the wind shifts again and whips it out of our goalie's hands. And it's gone in! It's 7 to the nothing. Even the wind is playing against us. There's no justice! There's no fairness. The referee's whistle blows. This soaking stupid sodden game has sucked from start to finish. When even the weather is whacking you in the guts, what chance is there?

Our team retreats for the changing room. And I look up at the sky, for answers. And I am speechless. I am Jamal, on Twitter, Insta and everything else. Me, Jamal, I'm lost for words. 7 to the nothing. Another crushing defeat. We just can't get a break. Even the wind's against us. Podcast 873.5. Jamal. I'm speechless.

I feel guilty about not being on the team.

THE UNDEAD, DEVILS & ROTTING FISH

The school got Black History Month mixed up with Diwali so Black History Month is now happening in December. Two classes – about sixty of us – are in the gym, ready for the Visiting Zulu Warriors of South Africa.

Yet instead of a dozen African dancers in fur skirts shaking spears, one Nike tracksuited guy strolls in. I recognize him as the samba guy me and Sheba met when we were doing the germ leaflets. The school dance teacher strides in after him and explains in a big voice that due to visa problems at the airport, the Zulus weren't able to enter the country; however, Mr Shaka has agreed to cover for them. She asks for a round of applause for Mr Shaka.

We clap as instructed. The dance teacher then heads to the back of the studio where she sits at a table, her head hidden behind a wobbly stack of exercise books.

We've had double maths after dreary assembly so we're ready to bust some moves. Half of us are already free-styling. Mr Shaka starts clicking his fingers in the air. Everyone copies him. The noise drops till it's only clicking you can hear.

111

'And stop,' he says. 'Raring to dance?'

'Yeah!'

'Anybody go to a Caribbean carnival this summer?'

About twenty people put their hands up and cheer. The dance teacher in the corner coughs loudly because she doesn't like cheering or any other expressions of joy unless it's part of a dance.

'Being a humble guy, I'm not going to boast that I had a band at Notting Hill Carnival and we won Best Dancers, Best Costume Design, Best Queen and Best Prince. But we did!'

We all jeer at his backhanded boasting. He keeps in perpetual motion as he talks, as if there's some music in the air that only he hears.

'Anyone heard of Blue Devils?'

Eddie puts his hand up so fast it almost shoots out of its socket. 'Me!'

'Go on then,' says the dancer, mock-scornfully.

'Is it like the Smurfs – because they're blue?'

'The Smurfs it is not, though we do have a Smurf move. Everybody ready? Right, feet together, copy me.'

He glides his right foot while dropping low, then comes back up high as his left foot slides to close the gap.

'That's the Smurf. And the other way …'

We glide the other way so we're back where we started.

'Now both – right then left.'

We do the moves.

'I can tell we're going to get on, you guys got moves already!'

This sets off a few more seconds of free-styling craziness, till he gets us clicking again.

'OK, quick background. The Blues Devils were Africans, placed on a slave ship and being taken to the Caribbean to be worked to death on sugar plantations. They jumped overboard to escape – and this is the magic – they didn't drown. Instead, they walked along the bottom of the ocean right back on to land. They touched land not as human beings, but as zombies. As Blue Devils. And they terrified people because they were out to take revenge for their ordeal. Everybody with me so far?'

'So it's a zombie dance, sir?' someone shouts.

Before he can answer, everyone starts busting zombie moves – because who doesn't love a zombie dance?

'Yes, the Blue Devils Zombie Dance!' he cries. 'We're going to do the "coming out of the water" move first. Everybody with the programme?'

He does a head-roll and side flick-kick. I copy it straight away.

'That boy there,' he says, pointing at me, 'come up, come up. We've met, haven't we?'

I'm embarrassed, but I go up and stand next to him.

'Maybe.'

'Weren't you a big dummy cheese at the Square?' He mimes me careering around in my costume. Everyone laughs. It doesn't trouble me.

'Yeh. An amoeba,' I say.

'You had moves. Both of you. Is the girl here?'

Sheba steps forward.

'Brilliant. You two can be my assistants for this session. Stand either side. We almost got arrested together, didn't we?'

At the back, the dance teacher's head picks up.

113

'Only joking!' he calls out to her. 'Now let's nail this dance!'

With his boom box laying down a background beat, he teaches us six different moves. The Slime. The Hold-Two-Sheep-by-the-Ears. The High-Stepping-Limbo. The Meat-Meets-Meat. The Fried-Chicken-Wipe and lastly, the Three-Severed-Heads-That-Roll-Roll-Roll.

It's tricky at first putting all the moves together but the boom box keeps us in time. After twenty minutes, we're all sweating and gasping though loving the moves. Mr Shaka calls a break.

'OK, everybody down, sit down, catch your breath. Anybody got questions, ask away. Any questions under the sun. Doesn't have to be about dance.'

Mr Shaka sits cross-legged and spreads his hands out on the floor. I imagine his palms pressing into the crumbs from a thousand lunch-boxes, the bitty rubber that the mats leave behind, the tears of the kids who've fallen off the gym rope, the blood of those who didn't make it over the vaulting horse. That floor.

Mr Shaka pulls at his nose twice. The sweaty smell down here must be hitting him.

'How long did it take you to learn to dance?' someone asks.

'Fifteen years and still learning.'

'What's the capital of Rome?' asks someone else.

'Italy, but the other way round.'

I put my hand up. 'Why does our football team always lose?'

'Does your football team always lose?'

114

Everybody choruses, 'Yeh!' Followed by 'They're shit!' 'They're rubbish!'

'Who's on the football team here?' he asks.

Six hands go up. Me and Sheba put our hands halfway up.

Mr Shaka asks each player to say their name and why they think the team loses. There's a forest of hands. He points to each person in turn.

'Imtiaz. We don't train enough.'

'Michael. We need to be fitter.'

'Horse. Nobody listens to the captain. Headless chickens.'

'Are you the captain?' Mr Shaka asks him.

'Yup.'

'You sound like one. Next.'

'Jared. We've given up, lost our passion for the game.'

'Jamal. We were improving then three of our best players left. Including him and her.' He points to me and Sheba.

I don't like Jamal's tone. 'We were always substitutes,' I tell him. 'Anyway, you're not on the team so shut up.'

'I bust my eye-socket, that's why I can't play. But I'd bust my heart, my kidneys, every organ in my body, every hair on my head, every drop of sweat on my, my, my ...'

'Skin?' suggests Mr Shaka.

'Yeah, skin, to play if I could. Unlike you two faint hearts!'

Jamal keeps on. He's jabbing the air at us: 'You were becoming some of our best players. The Windmill was starting to organize the team with you in it – you were even training us better. You let us down!' He turns to the others, and there's a lot of nodding confirmation from them. 'Quitters!' he hurls at me.

'Shut up, Jamal,' I tell him.

Jamal jumps up. 'Bring it!'

I'm on my feet, ready.

Horse gets between us, shouting, 'Lenny, let it go, leave it!'

I'm sick of Jamal and I push Horse, meaning to get him out of the way. Daft move. Next thing, Horse's head locks down into my chest. He tussles me to the floor though I manage to land a kick on Jamal as he jumps for me over Horse's back. He goes to punch me. I can see his bulging fist out of the corner of my eye but I can't move out of the way because Horse has me in a headlock. I scream. Horse twists and catches Jamal's fist in his hand just as it was about to land in my face. There's a gasp at Horse's strength. He forces Jamal back down on to the floor with the power of his hand alone. Sheba stops kicking Jamal's legs. This all happens in seconds.

Mr Shaka has bounced up. He taps Horse to release Jamal, which he does. Then Horse lets me go. I'm furious. At Jamal. At Horse. At everyone. Mr Shaka is in my face, talking to me.

'Look at me, not Jamal. Look at me. Eyes this way. Calm.'

I breathe.

'I can't sit with a quitter.'

It's Jamal, muttering. Mr Shaka looks over to him. 'You've got the gift of the gab, Jamal, I'll give you that. But enough now, right?'

Jamal turns away.

'So you were always a substitute, Leonard?'

'Yeh.' I look up. The entire team's looking at me with sour faces. I'm not scared of them. 'None of you know what it's like, waiting to be picked and you don't get picked week in, week out. Stuff that!'

'Yeh, who needs it when we can do drama!' Sheba jumps to her feet, doing jazz hands. Me and Sheba high-five.

Arguments break out everywhere.

Mr Shaka does more clicking.

'It sounds like this team's got issues,' he says. 'There's fight in you even if you're fighting yourselves at the moment. Your ideas are good. Train more. Listen to the captain. Help each other. Don't give up. You're at the bottom of the league, right?'

We all nod.

'You're the zombies of the League. So, do like the Blue Devils. Rise up. There's plenty of zombies in the world. Coffee pickers in Latin America. Cockle harvesters in Cumbria. Refugees blown halfway across the world by events outside their hands. Those are the modern zombies, on the sidelines, wondering "what if". And the story of the Blue Devils and their dance is: don't write these people off, don't write yourselves off. The Blue Devils rose out of the sea.'

'What's that got to do with us?' someone calls out.

'Why not rename your team the Blue Devils? There's another big team in Manchester called the Red Devils. So why not have Blue Devils? It's a strong name. Blue Devils! We can even put a dance to it!'

At the back, the teacher has woken up again. 'Mr Shaka, your Black History Month invitation is to teach dance, not politics. Can we have the children learning footwork please, not revolutionary theory?'

Mr Shaka mutters something to himself. He says out loud, 'Right, students, on your feet again. Ready? Let's go all the way through this time.'

He cuts the music almost instantly. 'Hold up, hold up!' He walks to the back where he stops by the dance teacher's table. 'Is Teach going to join in? Enough of marking homework, come on! Everyone give her a clap!'

It's a direct challenge. The clapping ramps up. Finally, she gives in. Everyone cheers.

She stands beside Mr Shaka so the line-up is now her, Mr Shaka, me and Sheba at the front, facing the class. I can see from the glint in Mr Shaka's eyes that this is going to be serious fun.

'Right, from the top … one, two, three!'

Something mind-blowing happens. Mr Shaka turns it on full, busting the moves slick and fast. We're all beat except the dance teacher. She matches him. He raises his dance game again yet still she copies him move for move. It's a dance-off.

Everyone forms a circle round them and starts clapping. Shake for shake, the dance teacher lives with him all the way. At the end, they break off and Mr Shaka says to her, 'I hereby declare you an Honorary Chief of the Blue Devil tribe!'

Later, I think to myself, we should have known she'd be good. She was a dancer in London before she started teaching.

Me and Sheba smurf, back-step, slime and limbo out of the school grounds. Neither of us wants to get home fast. We sit on a wall outside school. Sheba's looking at me strangely.

'What?' I ask.

'Didn't know you had a temper.'

'I don't.'

'Right.'

We sit there. Maybe I shouldn't have snapped at her. Maybe I shouldn't have let Jamal goad me. So many maybes, but it annoys me even thinking about him. Slowly I notice the sky. It's pinky-orange and fluffy.

'Look at the sky, Sheeb.'

'Like two pink elephants, smurfing,' she says.

I see it. Well, at least one elephant. The other shape is more like someone shaking a blanket. The street lights are blinking on and off. A British Telecom Broadband van goes flying past and the traffic snarls at the lights.

'Or a waterfall of roses.'

I look up and I get it. I get her. We're kicking our heels in time on the wall now.

'Did you hear about the bomb that went off?' she asks.

'Come on, let's smurf,' I say. I don't want to talk about bombs and stuff.

She stays on the wall.

A man in a Death Metal hoodie and black jeans has been leaning on the wall next to Sheba. He lights a cigarette. Sheba's phone rings and she starts talking; it sounds like her sister's checking up on her. The man's smoke clouds over Sheba as she talks on the phone. She stares at him and breaks the smoke cloud with a hand. He blows another cloud over her. She's off the phone now, and riled.

I tug at her. 'Sheba, come on, leave it.'

Reluctantly, she walks with me away from him.

I do a head-roll. It doesn't amuse her.

'Sometimes I hate people. Why did he pick on me?'

'Forget it, you're bigger than him.'

She blows a raspberry. 'He was huge.'

We stand by a lamp-post, not talking for a bit, looking at the tarmac.

She's still upset.

'Come on. I'll race you to the shop!'

We run halfway up the road, till we're shattered. She bends over, her hands on her knees. Then twists so she's looking at me upside down, sticks her fingers in her mouth and pulls a face. She's back.

We go into the shop and come out with a Twister lolly each.

'Hey, Sheeb, what did your fam say about the show – have you told them yet?'

She locks down and comes up in the squelch move.

'That bad?' I ask her.

'Only joking. It's all good. I told Grandma first. If she says no, nobody goes against her in the family. So I said to her, "Hi, Nana, I've got some news."'

'"What news, child?"'

'"I might be dancing in the school musical."'

Sheba's acting as her grandma now, hand clutching a stiff back, shaky knees bending.

'She had to put her teeth in, so she didn't speak at first. Then she tried to get out of her chair. I thought she was reaching for her slippers because usually she throws them at people if she's unhappy. She gets upright … and you know what she does next?'

'No, hurry up – what?' She's such a storyteller, Sheba, she always leaves you hanging.

'She starts dancing!' Sheba exclaims. 'Like shuffling her feet and warbling some old Punjabi song! Mum hears and comes in the room, amazed. Everyone comes in. Everyone's so happy. She's been miserable for ages.'

'So did your mum and dad say yes?' I quiz her.

She nods. 'Anything that makes Grandma happy is a good thing. Mum's going to find the old-time Punjabi tapes from the loft and play them for her every Saturday evening. She was so happy she cried.'

Sheba's spotted a bus she can catch. 'See ya!' She sprints off.

It's funny. When Sheba's gone I feel empty.

I only just settle into this thought when Eddie comes running up.

'You won't believe this!' He's shuffling and whooshing and spinning.

I try to slow him. 'Stop! Eddie! Eddie, Eddie. Why? What? What?'

Eddie gushes it all out.

'The Windmill's told me if I come back, I'm guaranteed to play because two more players have dropped out and it's all because of the diving – the referees were on to us. The first match, six of our players got booked and two of those got sent off for unsporting behaviour. Next match, two more sent off and the referee has a set of cards with numbers written on them from 1 to 10 and he gave ratings for performance. The Windmill had to tell everyone to stay on their feet no matter what happened.

'It was a nightmare. They lost 18:0 and some boys actually cried on the school van home. After everyone got off the van there was a real fight – with blood – between Horse and Marcus on one side and four other boys including Jamal, who only came for the ride. Horse bust all four boys' heads and now there isn't a football team and I'm picked. It's brilliant!'

The way Eddie trembles with excitement when he says all this, I know he's bailed from drama for good.

He finishes it up: 'It's my one chance. I'm no good at theatre. I can do the dance moves but I can't sing. Don't you see? It's now or never.'

He starts singing Elvis's 'It's Now or Never'. His singing would have even an audience of corpses fleeing. I beg him to stop.

'It's cool, Eddie,' I say. 'You have to … what's that expression?'

'Follow your dreams?'

'No.'

'Hit a man when he's down?'

'No. Seize the day.'

'Right.'

And I reflect on how one person's misfortune is another person's chance for glory.

Although it was a lot of words, Eddie has run through all this in maybe only a minute. His bus arrives almost the moment after he finishes telling me the news, and I'm back to being on my own.

At home, Mum is running around asking which cat has dragged rotten fish into the house. My sister Carla's playing footsie with her boyfriend, Gary, with one foot, powering her sewing machine with the other foot, while both of her hands are feeding fabric into the sewing machine's mouth. Meanwhile, Mustapha's got six crates on the living-room floor and is trying and failing to stack

122

them so he can carry them all at once to his van parked outside.

Nobody notices me. This is what I put up with.

I remember this morning's algebra lesson. *Simplify.* I help Mustapha carry his crates to the van then wave him off. One gone.

I get back in. After a suitable pause, I say to Carla's boyfriend, 'Was that your sister I saw you holding hands with last Saturday?'

'Yeh, absolutely,' the boyfriend says. He stumbles up as if he's suddenly remembered an urgent appointment and starts pulling on his shoes.

My sister's sewing machine stops. Her eyes follow her boyfriend's every move like a sniper getting their range.

'Since when did you have a sister?' Carla finally fires.

'She was poorly, she could hardly walk,' the boyfriend stammers. 'Babes, I got to go, I'll explain later.'

The boyfriend's out the door.

I settle down on the sofa. Somewhere inside myself I smile an evil smile.

Mum slams back in. 'Who's brought fish home?'

'Mum, it's not fish, it's the hypnotist,' I tell her.

'What are you burbling about?' she says.

'He's made you think the smell of cigarette smoke is rotting fish.'

'Why the hell would he do that?' Mum's eyes are still scanning the room for dead fish.

'To stop you smoking. Duh.'

She puts it together for the nth time. 'Thinking about it, I've not touched a cigarette in weeks. I buy them, then yeugh ... So why am I smelling fish in here?'

'The smoke stained into the ceiling and walls, maybe?'

'You mean I have to redecorate?' She's unconvinced. She looks around again. 'Are you smelling fish?' she asks me.

'I'm smelling cat pee. Stop chasing the cats around the house thinking they've brought home fish, you're scaring them.'

Mum ignores me. 'Carla. Are you smelling fish?'

Carla ignores Mum. 'Did you really see him with another girl?' she asks me. She's been stone-still ever since Whatsisname left in a hurry.

'Yeh,' I say, 'and she looked the spit of him. Like maybe they were twins.'

Carla breathes easy again. 'But why didn't he tell me?'

'Who knows?' I say. The evil part of me is rolling on the floor laughing but I sit there with my best choirboy face.

'Carla. Rotting fish?' Mum demands.

'No, thanks, Mum. I'll just have shepherd's pie if that's OK with you.'

Mum storms out into the kitchen. 'You two!'

I follow Mum. 'Fish, fish, everywhere!' she's saying.

'Mum, do you think we should go back to him and get it done properly?'

'Never!' Mum declares.

'Only I think my zombies are coming back. Everybody seems to be talking about zombies, the undead, devils, rotting flesh.'

Mum gives me her death-before-I-do-that look and says: 'It's just coincidence. You're not sleepwalking or anything and any spare money is going on redecoration costs, because if I have to scrub the fish out of the walls with a nailbrush then that's what I'll do!'

Whack! She slams a plate into the drainer for me to dry. Her teeth are locked together. I wonder if she needs to raise the nicotine level of her patches yet again.

I start whistling, which always calms her.

She tells me she's done eighty-five applications, had three telephone interviews and no job offers in the last three weeks. She swipes her eyes with a tea towel. I give her a hug.

Later, Mum serves us Middle East kofte. They're OK, but not as good as chicken burgers. Mustapha comes in and munches through the whole plate of them. He asks me what I did in school. I show him the dance moves. Mustapha lumbers a bit but he's not a bad dancer.

When I go to bed, all three cats follow me. I realize I know each step of the staircase by the noise it makes. From the short, high-pitched splintery sound of the first step through to the hollow long groan of the second step, all the way to the muffled cymbal of the final step. The cats ghost up without a peep.

All three sit on my bed as I'm trying to sleep. They've never done this before. It's weird. Oklahoma starts brushing her whiskers into my cheek. Another cat plucks at the quilt near my thigh. Darkness throws shadows over the room. It takes the cats a good fifteen minutes to settle down. I hear Mum tappety-tap in her heels up the stairs. Then Mustapha clumping up in his work boots, holding on to the banister, making it complain.

Mum's bare feet pad towards my door. She opens it, checking on me. The cats all look up. One of them hisses at her. I hear her gasp. She slams my bedroom door quick. *Serve her right for scaring them.* Eventually, all three cats start purring. The vibrations travel around the bed. It reminds me of the Wurlitzers at the fairground – dizzying but fun. I wish humans had a purr function. Then you could know more easily if they were happy or not. My *Philosophy Book* can't help with that. Instead, I read the football book, turning the pages by torchlight.

Mustapha clumps around, this time in the bathroom. I hear him using my electric toothbrush but I'm too tired to get up and shout at him. Soon, the only noise is Carla, downstairs. The doctor said the shock she got from the electricity left no burns on her because the electrics cut out, else she could have had a heart attack. She's sewing three giant cloth stars that a fashion house has ordered for a London fashion show. Her sewing machine runs in fast, smooth bursts. The same sound as a kung fu master doing a sword fight in his dojo. *Whoosh. Whoosh-whoosh. Whoosh. Drrr. Whoosh.*

Darkness wraps around my eyes like a cold bandage and I put the football book down. My breathing slips into the same rhythm as the cats' purring – it's like we're all one creature. Rain patters softly on the window, so softly it's almost not there. I hear the fading sound of an engine. In the distance, beyond the engine, beyond the muted swish of cars on the roads, is an echo of an echo of a football match. I see a foggy field. A team is playing there in the night, wearing ancient football kits. One turns to face me. His skin is brittle, crumbling. I struggle to get up out of bed. I can't. Something's on my face. Something wet. It paints wetness along my cheek and up to my eyelid then rubs my eyelid hard as if it wants to lift it and eat out my eyeball. I open the eye.

It's Oklahoma. Licking me awake.

'What are you doing, Okla?' I mutter.

I move her from my face and stroke her for a while.
All three cats are watching me.
Weird. They're guarding me, I realize.
I fall asleep.

EYEBALLS AND EARTHQUAKES

I wake up next morning to find I've had an avalanche of crazy texts from Jamal, Kwong, Marcus, Horse, even the goalkeeper.

If u say yes u can play on my PS4 – deal?

Bro we need u

Teams gonna be lit if u come bak

Believe in better

Keep the faith

At form class, Eddie joins in, giving it large about me not playing. The team's calling itself the Blue Devils now. Everyone's begging me and Sheba to pull on the shirt again. They've given up on the League but the Cup matches are starting next month.

'We want our A Team playing,' Eddie tells me, 'which means you and Sheba and not the reluctant fools Windmill rounds up with threats and bribes.' Eddie shakes me by the shoulders, urging, 'Say yes!' I laugh but say nothing.

More texts ping in all day.

We need you

Truce?

Ill do yr homework 4 u?

U can wear my spare boots

Ill give u a lift home on my bike
Cmon u know u want to
I'll take you to my barbers bro

It's a good feeling. Sheba's been getting the same. We show each other our texts when we meet up at Drama Club.

'My phone's been melting,' I tell her.

'I got a new ringtone. Mine's been laughing like a hyena all day. Wanna hear it?' Sheba plays her phone's text message alert for me. 'It's got me a detention for next week,' she says proudly.

We're in Warm-ups, stretching our fingers. We lock fingers.

'How's you and Jamal?' she asks.

I shrug. 'He don't talk to me and I don't talk to him.'

'You should make up,' she says, but when I don't respond, she leaves it.

Mr Sax sets the first exercise. It's called Space Station Fire! We lie in pairs on the gym floor, the top of our heads touching. We have to use crackly radio voices. Me and Sheba do the voices and the space station creaking but we chat about what we want unless Mr Sax nears, when she throws in phrases like 'pass me the radar gauge' and 'two degrees flick on the aspect comfort ratio' to please him.

The gazing game is next. You have to sit cross-legged opposite your partner, close your eyes and when Mr Sax shouts, 'Go!' open your eyes and gaze at them without talking or excessive blinking.

I look at Sheba's eyes as she looks steadily back. I see the black pupils at the centre of them. We're so close I have to refocus my eyes and choose only one of her eyes to look at. There's a circle of brown surrounding the black. The brown is flecked with different shades – like if you mixed brown with a bit of yellow, then a bit of green, a bit of red, a bit of blue. They're mainly rubber-band brown with the strands all moving. The surface of the eyeball catches reflections from the gym lights. Gazing at them, I feel this emotion that makes my stomach queasy.

Sheba tilts her head forward so her eyes become even bigger and the whites whiter. Her eyelashes swish down then up like car windscreen wipers. She sighs and shuffles closer to me so our knees are squished together. She gazes back at me. I can see my eyes in hers. It's like that mirror trick where you see a reflection of a reflection of a reflection …

'Keep going!' Mr Sax calls out.

This close, her eyes scare me. Then they fascinate me. Then they confuse me. Now they amaze me.

The gym's gone quiet with everybody eyeballing one another. It's like a junior opticians' magic ball.

'OK, I'm going to shout out some emotions and I want to see them in your eyes. Keep gazing!

'Murderous!' Mr Sax shouts.

Sheba bares her teeth and raises her hands to strangle me.

'Angelic!'

I put my hands together to make two wings, beating. Sheba stretches her neck, lifts up her chin and sucks in her cheeks.

'Flatulent, but no actual farts, please!'

He must have known what would happen. There's an outbreak of fake farting that spreads like a ripe hurricane across the gym. He hurries us on.

'OK. Amazed. And remember, no words!'

We both shake our heads and put our hands to our mouths in mock astonishment.

'Finally, let's try harmonious – a deep-seated feeling of contentment in another's company.'

It's then, looking into Sheba's eyes, that I realize what we have together. Harmoniousness.

As soon as the gaze session is over, it's break-time. Our phones start to ping. What to do? We agree we're not giving up Drama Club. Not while we're in the middle of rehearsals for the play.

Mr Sax catches us whispering. 'What skulduggery are you two plotting? Not about to burn the school down, are you?'

'Worse, sir – we're going to get the whole football team to see the musical,' Sheba tells him.

'Lord Have Mercy!' Mr Sax exclaims, then: 'Carry on – sell those fakers as many tickets as you can!'

We work out a text and then send it off to everyone in a four-thumbs flurry. The terms are: if the entire football team come to our musical, then, once the show is over, we'll both go back to the football.

'We don't negotiate,' Sheba insists. 'It's our way, or the highway!'

Our phones light up with replies. We make a pact to not read any of them till late at night. That pact lasts until we're about ten minutes past the school gates, then we can't help but look.

Everyone's agreed.

Sheba leaps on the wall and clenches both fists. 'Victory!'

131

The image of Sheba leaping around on the wall stays in my mind and I'm in a good mood all the way home. Then, as usual, someone spoils it.

I'm tired from walking. I open the front door and I sniff the air, trying to guess who's in, what's cooking and whether Mum's been chasing the cats again. I take two steps into the living room. Immediately I get ear-ache from Mustapha. He's standing in the middle of the room with a can of room deodoriser, frowning. No *hello*, no *how was your day?* from him.

Instead it's: 'Look what a mess you've made on the floor!'

I look. There's some tiny flecks of mud from my shoes. I think, What's his problem? He's making out like I've ridden a muddy bike round the room for hours or something. I ignore him, get rid of my bag and try to go find my mum. He blocks my way to the kitchen and starts again.

'Excuse, son, you've thrown your bag on the sofa, just after I've cleaned it.'

I've had enough. 'I'll throw it where I like,' I tell him. 'And I'm not your son!'

His voice drops to a cold whisper. 'I'm warning you, Leonard. Move your bag off the sofa. Now.'

'Or what are you going to do about it?' I sit on the sofa, pat my bag and dare him.

He cracks. 'That's it. I've had enough.' He flings the aerosol in a chair and slams himself out of the house.

Mum comes in. 'What was that?'

'He keeps calling me son,' I tell her. 'He's not my dad.'

'As good as.'

'He's not. Where's my real dad? Why don't you ever tell me?'

132

Mum sighs her I-don't-like-talking-about-this sigh. She sits next to me and takes my hand in hers. 'He's not good for you.'

I pull my hand away. 'Why did he leave? What was his sin?'

'Don't be cheeky.' She shuffles up next to me. 'Look at me,' she says. 'There's no need to be so upset.'

'The question, Mum.'

Mum blows her nose and her eyes roll back, remembering. 'He was really happy when I had you and Carla … but he wanted to put you in a boarding school.'

'What's one of them?'

'Where you stay in school all term. Of course I said no – it'd break my heart not to see you and anyway, we couldn't afford it. Then he wanted for us all to move to Black River, Jamaica, where he grew up. I didn't want to and there was no way I was giving you two up. So he left to work on the oil rigs. He's a stubborn man. When he doesn't get his way, he's off.'

'Mustapha says when people say someone's working on an oil rig it means they're in jail.'

'Mustapha's wrong. Your dad came over to study Engineering. He was a seismologist. Studied earthquakes. After his degree he took a job on a big dam project in France. Then he went to Aberdeen to work on the oil rigs offshore. How do you think they get the oil out? It takes science. Engineering.'

'If he's working on oil rigs and that, how come we're not rich?'

'He's worked on oil rigs all over the world so *he* probably is rich. But he's still upset because I didn't let him take you two to Jamaica so he won't give me any money.'

'He's been upset for fifteen years?'

'Yeh. Daft, isn't it?'

'And he never asks about me? Or Carla?'

'I'm sure he thinks about you. I'll get in touch with him, if you want. As you say, fifteen years is long enough. Would you like that?'

I say nothing because I can tell from Mum's tone that she doesn't want me to say yes.

Mum sails on. 'Anyway, there's no need to go shouting at Mustapha. He's a good man so please don't drive him away. Apologize to him.'

'Why?' I'm thinking it should be the other way round.

Mum gets exasperated. 'Because I say so!' She gets up, there's the smell of burning from the kitchen. Mum curses.

'He's gone,' I say.

'No, he hasn't. He's sitting in the car outside. He's texted me. Go and apologize. I'm not arguing with you. Go now.'

It's unfair but I do what Mum wants. I go outside. Mustapha's sitting in the driver's seat of Mum's car, eyes closed. His face looks like an old clay mask. I get in the car. He peeps open an eye and looks at me. I'm still angry with him.

'All right?' he says.

I nod. 'How's your eyebrows?' I ask.

'Growing back.'

I say it. The word that sticks in my throat: 'Sorry.'

'It's OK. It's just a habit – calling you son.'

'Habit? You've got children of your own?'

'Two. I *had* two boys. Twins.'

'Where are they?'

'They died in a fire in Germany. It was a long time ago.'
He takes out his wallet and shows me a photo. They look about five years old.

I don't know what to say, except: 'They look nice.' I look across. A tear's spilling from his eyebrow-less eye. Just one.

'I'm sorry,' I say. And I mean it.

'Not your fault,' he goes, shaking his head a little and stroking the steering wheel.

I don't know what to say again. We sit there a while, not talking. He wipes his eyes with the back of his hand. I think of something.

'I'll mop the floor.'

He nods. 'The bag doesn't matter,' he says. 'I was in a bad mood, drove a wrong way when I was delivering … You ever seen the Incredible Hulk?'

'The green muscles guy who rips his T-shirt. Like Superman but angrier?'

'Yeh.'

'I think so.'

'You're like that when you're angry, Lenny. "Aargh!"' He wipes his eyes again. 'Let's go inside. It's cold in this car.'

No sooner have I finished mopping the floor than Carla traipses in, flinging bags everywhere and muddying everything we've just cleaned. Me and Mustapha do a double-take at the wrecked floor.

'What are you two staring at?' Carla says.

Me and Mustapha are leaning into each other killing ourselves trying not to laugh. 'Nothing,' I tell her. 'Just life.'

I eat spaghetti with Milanese meatballs, which is OK, then I go to my room, to do my homework and punishment stuff.

In the middle of the day, the English teacher punished the whole class for excessive talking. We have to write five hundred words on *Whether it is the taking part that counts or whether winning is everything.* I've got no ideas at all, so I read three whole chapters of the *Philosophy Book*, then knock out an essay on my phone as I lie in bed:

There can be no winners without losers. Our team always loses. This means we have always given others the buzz of winning. Therefore, the applause at the end of the match is ours as much as the winning team's. Without us losing, they would not have won. As Socrates may have said, the other team may have the answer, but we are the question, and questions are important. I will now list the benefits of losing.

Winning does not test character as much as losing:

Can you avoid despair after multiple defeats?

Can you avoid swearing at your teammates or beating them up when they play really badly?

Can you trudge like a zombie from game to game knowing that at each game you're going to be thrashed and laughed at?

Can you get over your defeat, pull your kit on one more time, knowing the same thing's going to happen again – that your destiny is to lose and lose again?

Winners have different feelings to losers. They must feel lots of words beginning with E: Euphoric. Ecstatic. Excellent. Elated. Maybe even Elastic. They want to jump for joy. Sometimes they can't. Why? Because the losers are still on the pitch and it would look like you were rubbing their noses in it if you started chest-

bumping while the losers were dragging their sorry feet to the changing rooms. That's why losers should get off the pitch as fast as possible, so winners can celebrate without feeling awkward. This is called magnanimity.

I stop writing at this point because all three cats are attacking my toes and I have to chase them out of my bedroom.

I was going to look at the football book next but I'm too tired. I lie back and doze off, trying to avoid thinking of zombies by only thinking of pleasant things. I remember this afternoon.

Me and Sheba were walking through the park, our phones still pinging, when she suddenly said: 'You stared so looong into my eyes!'

I started to explain how I saw the curve of the eyeballs and the way her pupils go bigger and smaller and how the eyelashes close, but she interrupted me: 'No. I mean, what did it feel like here?' She goes to tap my heart, but I turn away out of reach.

'Well?' she persists.

'Strange. I always thought your eyes were one brown colour but they're not, they're made up of stripes that are all different shades, sitting next to each other. Like toothpaste stripes.'

'My eyes are like toothpaste?'

'They're beautiful.'

'You really mean that?' She was looking across at me when she said this.

I remember feeling embarrassed and getting hit by that stomach lurch I'd felt on the Wurlitzers. I waited for the feeling to go. Then I turned and said, 'Yeh. I like toothpaste.' The trees in the park all shook in the wind.

Sheba's eyes hid a grin. Her phone suddenly hyena-ed which made us both laugh. She jumped up on a wall.

I'm lying in bed, remembering all this when suddenly this noise starts from the bathroom.

Dzzzzz.

This time I'm ready. I bounce out of bed, storm into the bathroom and snatch my electric toothbrush off Mustapha. He mumbles a foamy apology but I'm not interested. 'Sorry, is this yours?' does not cut it. I tell him a million of his germs will be buzzing round my mouth now if I use it so he has to buy me a new one. *Eugh.* Mum comes into the bathroom and for once agrees with me. I stomp back to bed. I can't sleep, I'm so annoyed.

Somehow Oklahoma has sneaked in and is purring on the window-ledge. She comes and sits on my pillow, pushing her furry face into mine. I move her but she always comes back to the same position. I give up. She purrs. *Prrrr. Prrrrr Prrrrrr.* All night long.

This is what I put up with.

MUSIC AND MISERY

Romeo & Juliet: The Musical
Story by William Shakespeare
Songbook by Gordon Sax
Additional Music by Ms Clare S. Podborsky
Costumes by Carla Blackwood
Cast: to be announced

After three weeks of rehearsals, *Romeo & Juliet: The Musical* is coming together. It's a mash-up of two Shakespeare plays, *Romeo and Juliet* and *As You Like It* which, Mr Sax tells us, is the one where everyone runs off into the forest, gets dressed up as someone else and then they all fall in love with the wrong people.

There aren't many spoken lines in our musical. Instead it's packed with song and dance. We're doing Hip-Hop, Contemporary, a zombie dance and ballet.

Sheba is the star in rehearsals. She's in a group of five girl gymnasts who are all super-flexible. After every rehearsal, Sheba and her gymnast friends stroll out, while I stagger, my legs throbbing with solid pain. I'm usually so exhausted that when I get home, I crawl into bed and sleep as stiff as an Egyptian Mummy.

Though the dance is tough, the singing is tougher. There are so many songs to learn, and you have to sing them in different voices depending on whether you're a girl or a boy at that point in the plot. I have to sing in a high-pitched voice called falsetto when I'm a girl.

We have separate lessons for the singing. The technician in the school's recording studio tapes your singing, plays it back for you and then we listen for errors. Sometimes we do the same song twenty times in a session. I have to learn scales, how to use my stomach muscle (where the sound starts), and where to put my chin when I sing big notes – stuff like that. It's hard work. I was there singing during break one time and I opened my eyes at the end of this song and there was a whole class outside, clapping me.

When I sing my first falsetto song at Drama Club, most of the boys wet themselves laughing. But Mr Sax tells them just how many male singers have sung it – including Prince, Justin Timberlake and Frank Ocean – and how hard it is to do it well. 'Leonard Blackwood is not good, he's brilliant!' Mr Sax tells them. He challenges them to a sing-off with me. They all go quiet.

At the end of the rehearsal Mr Sax hands me a note for my sister. He's asked her to do the show costumes.

Time flies. After we finish rehearsing, Mr Sax waves me and Sheba over. 'I've decided!'

'Decided what, sir?' Sheba asks.

'You two. That's my decision.'

'You mean we ...?'

'Yes.'

Sheba screams then flings herself into a cartwheel. I come round from doing a back-flip and we hug it out. We're now leading girl and leading boy.

Everyone in the gym is clapping but only politely. I guess there's a lot of envy out there.

'That means practice,' Mr Sax exhorts us. 'I want a spec-tac-u-lar performance from both of you. Understand?'

Walking home is like flying. We do all the dances. At the bus stop we do the songs. On the bus we bust zombie dance footwork since it fits with the lurches of the bus. Everyone on the number 192 breaks out into zombie lurching and we sing the zombie song over the top of it. It's the ride of a lifetime. The bus driver claps as we get off, then she calls us over and asks where can she get tickets.

Two weeks before the show, I look up from my cornflakes to find my sister handing me a large sealed envelope with her designs in. She says she'll kill me if I open the envelope before I get it to Mr Sax – and as she says it, she has killer eyes. She's tired from having stayed up all night drawing, I guess.

I keep the envelope in my locker during classes but just as we're gathering outside the gym for Drama Club, Sheba wrestles it off me. I try to wrestle it back and it splits. Mr Sax scoops it up off the floor and carries it aloft into the gym. Everyone crowds round. He throws off what's left of the envelope and reveals Carla's costume designs, page by page, describing them for everyone.

'We begin in the oceanic greens and blues of our sunken heroes of blue devilry. Very Paul Smith, for the boys especially.' He holds the page up.

141

There's gasps. Oohs. Aahs.

'We are then transported to the clean elegant lines of the Russian ballet, with ornately frilled cream tutu and lilac tunic for Her and the most elegantly rising green tights and sparkling royal green and gold doublet for Him. Together, a wondrous, balletic charm.' He holds up that page.

Sheba will look amazing. I get that. But me? I'll be wearing green tights. And I'll have what looks like a sock stuffed down the front. There's giggles. Soon the boys are rolling around, throwing out jokes like 'Don't worry, Leonard, it's no biggie' and all kinds of weak jokes like that. *Why did Carla design me this?* I fume. Hot-faced, I clench my fists, trying to ignore the mockers.

Mr Sax flicks through a few more designs. 'Now what have we here? Ah, Leonard, next is your dress, I see.'

The giggles start up again.

'But what a dress. Disguised as a girl in this, what boy would not fall for you? A diaphanous creation with a fetching stretch to the salmon Lycra panels and an enchanting spangly silver bustle to set off your derriere. You will surely be the belle of the ball in this!' He holds the design up.

I didn't understand a word Mr Sax said and I know he's winding me up but the dress doesn't actually bother me. I'm cool with it, I tell myself. Or I was until one clown has one giggle too many. I aim a punch that would have flattened him if he hadn't ducked. Then I slam him to the floor and sit on him. Mr Sax drags me off.

'Leonard, Leonard, save the drama for the stage!'

He makes me and the boy sit three metres apart. I look around, ready for anyone else. The giggles die off.

Walking home, it's still sinking in. *I can't believe Carla's put me in tights. My own sister.* Sheba tries to calm me down with a whole long list of reasons.

'Who cares? It's Shakespeare and that's what they wore in those days. You'll look good in them. If anyone can pull it off, it's you. You'll look cooool.'

I'm not convinced. 'Nice try, Sheba, but I've been set up. It's because I lied to her about her boyfriend having another girl on the go. This is her revenge.'

'The tights?'

'Yeh.'

'Not the dress?'

'The dress doesn't bother me.'

'I don't understand.'

'There's four boys wearing a dress. I'm the only one in green tights showing off my nuts.'

'Seriously? It's not like you're knock-kneed or got fat thighs like me.'

'You haven't got fat thighs.'

'Now *you're* being nice … Really?'

'Definitely not got fat thighs.'

She pushes the ring-pull into the can she's fished out of her bag and offers the can to me. I take a swig and pass it back. The can goes back and forwards between us till she reaches her turn-off road. At this point, she runs off. Sheba never actually says goodbye when we part, just dashes. I have no idea why.

I get home and I can tell Carla's in because I can smell her as soon as I open the door. I slam my way through to the living room and throw my bag on the sofa.

'Temper, temper.'

I look across at her.

'What's up, little brother? Somebody smoked your fish?'

'Don't nobody mention fish in this house!' shouts Mum from the kitchen.

'What kind of madness are those designs?' I ask her, collapsing on to the sofa. 'Everyone's laughing at me.'

'There's nothing fishy going on at all,' Carla says.

'Carla, I've told you! No fish!' shouts Mum.

This is what I have to put up with.

Carla is behind her machine, sewing thick, Elizabethan-style jackets. There's cloth, zips, buttons, threads and sewing machine spare parts everywhere.

'Ingratitude,' she mutters. Then she gasps as a needle goes through her thumb. She dashes off and I hear her run water over her thumb under the tap in the kitchen. She comes out again and slumps into the mountain of cloth on her machine.

There's a noise coming from her corner of the room and I can't tell if she's sobbing or if she's just not taken her foot off the sewing-machine pedal.

'Here I am, a human pin-cushion for you lot and all I get is complaints!' she finally wails.

'Why put me in tights though?' I say, but more gently than before.

She picks her blurry face up quick as a flash. 'Is that what this is about?'

'Yeh.'

'It says ballet on the script. Anything other than tights would be like … a fish out of water.'

'Carla, I'll gut you!' shouts Mum.

'Look, I've done your stuff first. Why don't you nip upstairs, try it all on and then you'll see. I even got you one of these.' She comes out from behind the machine,

144

rummages through all the material on the floor and holds something up.

'What's that?'

'A dancer's belt. It goes at your front and makes everything … even.'

She holds it out. It's a green jock strap. It's still in its plastic box. She dives back into the pile of material and starts flinging other things out. 'Here's your jacket. Your leggings. Shirt. Try it all on. Go. Then come down and show me.'

Reluctantly I gather it all up in my arms, go upstairs and lock the bathroom door.

When I look in the mirror, it all fits OK. Still. I come down wearing it. Immediately Carla starts plucking at the jacket with her fingers and clucking over seams and stuff. She has me turn round and round.

'Um,' she says, 'have you got the dance belt on?'

I nod. I can feel its straps tugging up my bum crack.

'Your boxer shorts are spoiling the line. But it's up to you.'

Mum comes in from the kitchen and gasps.

'Oh my God, a prince out of a fairy tale. My baby! Oh Carla! Oh Leonard! Let me get a camera!'

I dash out of the room before Mum can start snapping. She'd put the photos on her Facebook and then the whole world could laugh, not just the entire school. I like seeing my mum happy though. It's rare. She's always worrying, if not about getting a job then about fish.

That night, I flick through my *Philosophy Book*, but there's nothing in it on how to handle humiliation or having to wear green tights. I bring up SoundCloud on my phone and listen to Jamal's latest podcast on the team. The team took a hammering. Jamal is brief and miserable.

Jamal's Podcast

14 nil. 14 to the nothing. We've been deserted by important players. We've been deserted by fate. If I sucked a straw all year I'd never see as much ... as much ... as much something as I've seen today. What are the missing words? Bad luck? Misfortune? Rain? Rancid passing? Rubbish refereeing? Take your pick. I've going to go dip myself into an ice bath to recover. I'm going to move abroad. I'm going to have to become a hermit. I can't take this any more. This is Jamal, The Speechless. On Twitter, on Insta and everything else. Podcast 873.5. I can't take any more. Jamal, The Speechless, signing off.

I feel sorry for them. I wonder how Eddie coped. 14:0 is an epic loss. I thumb through my dad's football book. They all wore baggy cotton shorts in the olden days. I pause at a photograph of a goalkeeper looking crestfallen as the scoreboard in the stands says 13:0. I imagine being the goalkeeper. The photo starts to glow. My body tingles. I hear the crowd's booing at the goalkeeper as he picks the ball out of the net. I can hear faint shouts coming from the park. *The zombies.*

Using every ounce of effort I can find in myself, I put the book down and chant to myself: *'There are no zombies. There are no zombies.'*

STAGE FRIGHT

Rehearsals go fast. A few people drop out because they can't hack it. Their replacements struggle because the play can get complicated. I overhear a conversation between Mr Sax and a new recruit.

'What am I again, sir?'

'You're a girl playing a boy playing a girl. Got it?'

Silence.

'So I start out as?'

'A boy.'

'Then I become?'

'A girl.'

'And then next scene I'm?'

'A boy.'

'Wait a minute, sir, I still don't get it.'

Big sigh. Silence.

'When the costumes come, you'll get it. Leonard, why are you hiding over there – and what are you sniggering about?'

I come out from behind the mountain of mats.

'I'm not and nothing, sir.'

'How's your sister doing with those costumes?'

'She's finishing them, sir. The zips and buttons and things.'

'Impress upon her the urgency of our situation. We are one week, I repeat, one week, away from dress rehearsal. We need them pronto.'

'Right, sir.'

When the full dress rehearsal comes up, I style out the tights. The truth is, everyone is too busy worrying about remembering their own lines and footwork to be looking at me. And I realize a simple truth that the *Philosophy Book* did say: In life, 99 per cent of the time, 99 per cent of other people are focused on themselves, not you, and even that 1 per cent who are looking at you don't last. By the second dress rehearsal, even I've forgotten I'm wearing the tights.

On page 87 of the script there are only two words:

[They Kiss]

That's it. In all our rehearsals so far, we've skipped that page. There's a really difficult *a cappella* duet song before it, and after it there's a big dance number where everybody's on stage. Page 87 is forgotten. That is, until one of the girls who dropped out of performing due to stage fright but who still wanted to be involved gets the job of prompter. She likes everything to be done exactly as it's written down.

When the *a cappella* song ends, we start to move into the big dance. She waves the script to stop the rehearsal and calls out: 'But it says here "They Kiss". You're missing out page 87, sir. "They Kiss"!'

Everyone groans. We're in a hurry.

Mr Sax flicks through the script. 'No, she's right, that makes total sense.' He looks up at me and Sheba. We're centre stage, catching our breath still after having belted out the song.

'Leading man, leading lady, how do you feel? A kiss here would give a real kick to the dance number that follows.'

I look across at Sheba.

It's the Romeo and Juliet scene. She's in a Juliet dress. I'm in the Elizabethan doublet and tights.

Everyone's waiting.

I feel the heat at the collar of my shirt and tingling in my hands. My lips are dry. I look again. She looks away so I can't see her face but I can tell she's not happy. It's in the arch of her back and the way her head's dropped. I feel the chafe of my shirt at my neck.

'Well, Sheba?' asks Mr Sax, checking his watch.

She turns and comes towards me, stubbing the toes of her feet with each step she takes.

'Stop,' Mr Sax says. 'Suddenly I'm not feeling it. Hug instead?'

I shrug.

'Or a smile. One sweet smile is worth a thousand words. What about that, Sheba, my star?'

'A hug's fine, sir. Like this.'

She bends at the waist, extends her arms around me. One of her hands finds my back. Two taps and she breaks. It's about as romantic as putting out the rubbish.

'Marvellous. Spell-binding!' says Mr Sax.

There's a banging. The cleaners are outside the gym, wanting to get in. Mr Sax scrambles: 'So, thespians, we've done the song, we've done the hug and now, positions please. On four into the dance: two, three, four!'

149

On the way home after rehearsal, Sheba's walking two steps ahead of me, her hands thrust in her trouser pockets. She's doing sighs. She does one that ends like a bird calling. Then the kind of lip sigh that sounds like blowing bubbles in water.

'What was that about?' I ask her.

'The kiss thing?' she replies.

'Yeh.'

'You're not all that. I'm not dying to kiss you or anything.'

'I know that.'

'So?'

I shrug. 'I didn't wanna do the kiss either.'

'Perfect.'

We've linked arms. It just happens. She does another sigh. An old man one. Then a goldfish one. She flicks her shoe lace in a puddle then back out. *Sigh. Sigh. Sigh.* We keep walking.

'But Sheebs, you hugged me like … I had a disease or something. Do I really make you feel that bad?'

She squints her eyes at me.

'I can tell you're hiding something,' I say. 'I know you.'

We've stopped walking.

'Look at me, Sheebs.'

Big, sad eyes turn up to mine. Right now, they have these amazing, flecked, rubber-band discs that are glossy like a lake in a forest of eyelash trees.

'How long am I supposed to keep looking at you for?' she says.

She always makes me laugh.

'Sheebs, I know you. There. You just flicked your eyes left then right. You do that when you're hiding something. C'mon. Spill the beans.'

'Promise you won't say "oh shit" if I tell you.'

'Promise.'

'I never really told my grandma I was doing the show. Now my sister is bringing her to see it.'

'Oh shit.'

She thumps me. 'She'll kill me. And she'll double kill me if she sees me kissing a boy.'

'Why is your sister even bringing her?'

'I don't know. To get her out of the house. Sis says she's gonna tell her it's a Duke of Edinburgh Award Ceremony and chances are, Grandma won't know any different because mostly she doesn't know what's going on around her, though now and again she understands everything. You can never tell.'

I'm amazed. 'You lied to me! What else have you lied about?'

She's still got hold of my arm. With her free hand she pokes me. 'What have *you* lied about? I've spilt my beans, you spill yours!'

I think of all the lies I've told Sheba. It's hard rounding them up, there's so many.

'Look at me,' she says.

I look at her lips. They're full and quick and the tip of her tongue peeps out of them when she gets wild like this.

'At my eyes, not anywhere else. Lenny, I can tell when you're gonna lie to me, you always wear this cheesy grin on your face. Lose the grin and tell me the truth.'

I think: My biggest lie is when I said I didn't want to do the kiss with her today. But I can't tell her that. Next biggest lie? When I said I don't think about her much when she's not with me. Further down on the list? That my dad's Thierry Henry. That I do fifty press-ups every night. All the lies about liking walking in the rain (unless she's with me). So many lies. Which one to fess up to?

She's poking me again. 'Are the zombies a lie?'

'No. I really did see them.'

'They've gone now?'

'Sort of.'

'What kind of answer's that? "Sort of"?'

She's threatening to poke me again so I grab her in a ballet hug. She's in my arms and comes up on her ballet toes and laughs, then wriggles so that's she's turned right into me. I'm looking into those lush brown eyes of hers and she's still for once. Her eyes are beautifully still, like pools you could dive into. Just then her bus pulls up and her friends on the bus start knocking like mad on the window, calling her. She runs off. I'm left alone, thinking, Buses always arrive at the wrong moment.

THE CURTAIN FALLS

This is it. The day has arrived. It's show-time! I throw off the covers, jump out of bed and look out of my window. The sun is pushing through. The neighbour with the wonky bike is wibble-wobbling back from the corner shop with a litre of milk. Oklahoma is biting my ankles, trying to get me to play with her. I pick her up. She squirms out of my arms but I catch her again. Mustapha is in the bathroom. I listen. He's not using my toothbrush. From the top of the stairs I smell frying oil. I go down.

Carla has left costume sets for twenty actors on two giant clothes rails that fill the living room. Seeing them all together, and all their different shapes and sizes, I realise how hard Carla's worked. She stopped over at her boyfriend's last night.

I sling the cat on to the sofa and rock into the kitchen. Mum sniffs my hair. She's making me fried eggy bread. I tell her to remind Carla to deliver the costumes in time. Mum says it's all sorted – a courier is picking them up at lunchtime.

I practise dance moves all the way to the school gates and beyond.

It's strange how sometimes the hands on a classroom clock can whizz round the clock-face and other times you want to go up there and shove them round yourself, you're so sure the clock is bust. The History teacher drones on and on. I wonder if they give the teachers extra lessons in how to be boring, how to turn any subject into something so tedious that even the mice in the school walls keel over and die a boredom-related death.

I feel myself slide lower in my chair. It's last lesson. I check with Eddie. 'Eddie?'

'What?'

'The show. You guys still coming?'

'Yeah. The Windmill's promised cakes to everyone after. I'm bringing my sis. Marcus is bringing his girlfriend, that'll be a laugh. Jamal's bringing his cousins and Horse is coming in a velvet suit. You'd better sing good, bro, 'cos we're paying top dollar for this. Ten quid a ticket.'

'You'll love it.'

'I wanna taster!'

The teacher's got her head in a laptop. I slide off my chair and quietly reel off a few lines from the Dancehall song. Eddie starts popping. The whole back row starts rocking. The teacher tells us to stop mucking about and get on with describing living conditions for the working poor in Victorian England.

This is my life.

The clock has finally waded through the millions of seconds that separated us from the home-time bell. It dings its joyful dong. A cheer goes up. We're free. There's a mad scramble for the door that no amount of teacher yelling 'Do Not Run!' can put the brakes on.

Like rats out of a sinking ship, everyone flings themselves in the direction of the exit doors. Except that in my case, I'm heading for the gym. Two hours from now, I'll be on stage. Will I remember my lines? Will I fall flat on my arse? Will I lose my voice, mid-song?

Mr Sax grabs me. 'What's with the long face, Leonard?'

I tell him.

And he tells me there is no reason on this earth to have such negative thoughts. 'You are a prince and your court awaits you out there. I ask only two things. One. Do your best. And two. Have fun. Don't worry, we'll catch you if you fall. Now get ready to swish out there and knock 'em dead!'

He wants to say more stuff like this but I say I need to check my costume again. He has me smiling though and suddenly I'm confident. He's a magic teacher – I don't know how he does it.

I'm climbing into my Scene One zombie outfit when Sheba rocks up.

'Hey, Leonard!'

'Yeh?'

'Break a leg.'

'Why would I do that?'

'It's tradition to say it.'

'It's stupid.'

'OK. I hope all your legs and things remain unbroken.'

'What d'you mean? Why are you looking at my tights?'

'I'm not.'

'Good. Help me get into this.'

She holds my shirt while I wrestle into the zombie outfit top that goes over the other stuff. Then she bear-hugs me. Just like that.

'What's that for?'

155

She doesn't answer. Instead, she runs off making spaceship sounds. Sometimes, I don't understand Sheebs.

The gym fills up. It looks like there's more people than seats at first but it settles until only the front row is empty. Mr Sax says that's normal in the theatre: nobody likes to be on the front row because you get a stiff neck there.

Backstage is cooking. Mr Sax gets us together and we do a final warm-up. We do hugs. We bump fists. Then everyone's tugging at their costumes, *doh ray me*-ing through their songs, shuffling their feet and chanting lines. Mr Sax goes round giving everybody little 'Good Luck' cards, usually with one word on it like 'Louder!' or 'Smile!' or 'Extend!'

The five-minute call comes through from the prompter. I whizz through my lines in my head and check myself in the mirror. In the first scene I wear my zombie costume, with tights underneath for a quick costume change into Scene 2, the ballet. I check that my dresser's ready for the clothes swap. Then I peep round the stage curtain and take a look at the audience.

Eddie and the footballers have trooped in and are sat on the back row. Horse is among them, looking fine in a purple velvet suit and black bow tie. My mum and Carla are in a middle row, my mum sniffing the air. Carla has a big beam on her face. I see Sheba's sister sitting with her mum and an old lady that must be her grandma to the side.

Mr Sax calls order. The lights go down. There's a hush. *It's now. It's happening.* The sack-clothed Storyteller goes on and does the intro:

This is not mere meaningless rhyme,
My voice rising says now is the time

To stick your chewing gum under your chair
And earwig this wondrous tale if you dare!

There's cheers from the back. The lights rise on the set. The Storyteller raises her voice again to set the scene:

'Before you, a splendid wood,
And an even more splendid estate.
Now enter this handsome youth
Desperately seeking a date!'

That's my cue. As the music ramps up, I bound on in my Blue Devils outfit and do a splits jump. I land it on the spot and segue into a body-pop that ends with me standing stock-still centre stage in a scarecrow hang. I nail it perfectly. Then I wink at my mum. The audience go wild. They're shouting my name. The back row goes nuts. I have trouble keeping my face straight but I manage.

The lights go fully down and the spotlight picks out the Storyteller again:

'His heart contains a yearning,
That keeps him up most nights,
But the girl who features in his dreams
Lives up thirty-six, death-defying flights!'

The Storyteller bounds off. Eerie music kicks in and the zombie force join me on stage in the stagger-out-of-water dance. We lock straight from that into the zombies-climbing-stairs routine. The whole audience goes wild. Calling out the names of dancers. Doing the dance moves with us. We ride it all out. We're slick. In synch. It's lit.

The scene ends in a big, raking graveyard move that leaves only me on stage. As the music fades, the lights black out. I duck behind stage, throw off my Devils rags to the dresser, slip into the doublet and check my tights. Meanwhile, the spotlight picks out Sheba on the balcony. On cue, she leans over:

'Romeo, Romeo, wherefore art thou, Romeo?'

The back row of the audience roars back: 'He's behind you!' 'Don't do it!' 'Jump!'

Horse leaps to his feet. 'This is theatre, not panto! Hush all of yuz with your "he's behind you". To raas!'

The Storyteller comes on quickly:

'If only they were in the forest,
Not in the city born,
They could dance to Debussy's
L'Après Midi D'Un Faune.'

I'm back on. Someone calls out: 'Look at them tights!' It's chaos in the audience again as everyone starts arguing.

In the wings, Mr Sax is frantic.

I do the ballet skips, arms held high in an oval shape, then move into a slow spin. I pause and look straight at the audience at the end of the first spin rotation. There's an instant hush. Then I spin again. Look again. Then spin faster and faster. I hear the cheers hitting the roof. I do the bow.

It's the *Sheba and her band* scene now. I watch from the wings. The costumes are Oliver Twist rags, but using bold colours. Someone puts the wrong track on. It gets pulled. The right track drops. Violins soar as a beat-box track solo follows it. Sheba's dancers hit the stage with crisp, sharp, Contemp moves, forming shapes and symmetry all over the floor. Then Sheba does a handstand flip–flap that ends in a soaring vault. They catch her mid–flight, spin her round and she climbs till they're holding her up by her legs. She sings her big number like that. It's the biggest number in the whole play and it brings the house down.

As the applause dies, the band surround Sheba, pretending to talk. I come on stage, rear left, in my Romeo costume. A spotlight picks me up. The actors around Sheba do stage whispers and point. Sheba sees it's me, but dismisses me – she's not interested. She proclaims:

'A girl of an independent mind has no real need of a guy.
All she needs is a library card, choccie and, of course, free wifi!'

The dancers surround Sheba saying, 'Go, on, go up to him, go on!' But she refuses. They lock step and the movement flows into a hip-hop dance.

I look across the audience. The football boys have lost their smirks and are glued to the dance. That's no surprise. What floors me is this: sitting on the front row, which has been empty for the first three scenes, are twelve zombie footballers. They're in their 1966 kit. They turn their skulls this way and that as the girls dance.

The zombies are back.

'Psst!' I call to Mr Sax in the wings. He comes over. I point them out. He can't see anything.

'But sir, they're there!' I hiss.

'Leonard, my star, now is not the time to lose it. Do your thing. You're doing brilliantly. The audience loves you, zombies and all.'

159

'I can't, sir!'

He takes my shoulders and pushes his face right close to mine. 'You can. Focus. Composure. Five seconds. Get the dress on. Go!' He slaps my back and I gallop to get in place in time. The big hip-hop dance number finishes.

Sheba waits till the cheers die off, then says:

'All a girl needs is a female companion.
We need boys like our breath needs onion!'

The stage clears. I'm back on, this time dressed as a girl. The audience erupts. I don't mind. I style it out, waiting for them to settle.

Sheba's remained on stage. It's the only time we're alone in the play. We go through our lines. I have one eye on the audience. My mum has her annoying, 'Oh isn't he cute!' look on her face. Carla looks like she's spotted a design flaw in one of the costumes and is itching to do something about it. The football boys have calmed down after the initial cat-calls. And the zombies … I don't look at the zombies.

Sheba's nudging me. It's my line. I say it, in character, as a boy pretending to be a girl:

'We are all beautiful creatures, whatever skin we wear.
Sisterly love is a beautiful thing, we have so many dreams
to share.'

We're into the big tear-jerker numbers. Sheba goes first and brings tears to everybody's eyes. She ends on:

'…so my heart will always be true!'

She holds the last note forever. Her applause doesn't die down for ages. I wait and wait. Finally, there's hush and it's time for my song. When I hit the first falsetto note, there's a titter from somewhere. A solitary titter. I carry on singing but the titter spreads like a fire. Horse gets up.

'I'm liking this. This is art. Let's hear it. Understand?'

Everyone goes quiet.

I pick the song up again. The audience settle into it. I see their faces softening. They're swaying. My mum's beaming with pride. Midway through, I feel my tonsils getting sore. I hold my chin down, my neck in the right position and relax my stomach so I can feel the vibration there. It works. I'm fine. I keep going. Finally, I hit the high note that ends the song.

There's absolute silence. Then slowly one clap becomes two which becomes four until they're all clapping like crazy.

When it's finally quietened down, the spotlight picks up Sheba and follows her as she comes towards me. I put my hands out. She's meant to hug me.

Instead she goes up on her toes.

And kisses me.

On the lips.

I'm stunned. Her lips are on mine. I move my own lips, kind of slide them across hers. She moves her lips as I move mine. We're kissing. We're actually kissing. There's all this noise. Cheers. Jeers. Clapping.

I open my eyes just in time to see a slipper, as if in slow motion, flying through the air. I hold out a hand to stop it, but it's too late. The slipper whacks Sheba on the shoulder. Then her grandma's up and shouting. There's chaos. Mr Sax calls from the wings. 'Keep going, keep going!'

The music for the next dance comes on. I remember me and Sheba are meant to do a costume change. I run to the wings, pulling Sheba with me. The entire cast is ready and we're back in three seconds in Blue Devils mode for the final number.

We stagger through it, limbs flailing everywhere, shoes slipping, some of us mixing up verse and chorus, but we do it, we cross the Finish line. It's done.

The Storyteller comes on for the last time:

'You have listened to our story
Old myths we did destroy
Love needn't end in tragedy
Sometimes it ends in joy:

When the right lass meets the right lass,
When the right lad meets the right lad,
And when the right girl falls in love with the right boy.'

We take a bow.
The curtain drops.

THE AFTER-LIFE

The after-party's cooking. Horse has shed his velvet jacket and is at the heart of all the jump-ups. Jamal's on the decks laying down his own craziness on top of the music. We dance five tracks one after the other then the sound-levels fade down.

'Let's hear it from the cast!' Jamal is calling on the mic. 'Let's hear it from the stars. Say some words, drop some lines, let them feel the love, come up! Come up!'

There's cheers. Everyone starts showing me to the mic. I'm looking for Sheba, but I can't see her anywhere. Jamal's crazy-making, having everyone wave their arms in the air and call my name.

'Hush!' Horse calls. 'Let Lenny speak!'

'Go for it,' Jamal says to me as he passes me the mic. We do a hug. It's the first time we've spoken since we fell out. He pushes me forward. My legs are aching. My throat's sore. Everyone's waiting.

'Is this live?' I ask Jamal. When the audience laugh at me, I know it is.

I try to get a thought together. 'What can I say?' I say into the mic. 'I'm so happy. I've made great new friends, and well ... so thanks to you all.' I come to a halt. It's not like there's a script. I'm dying here on the mic. Then I spot Mr Sax. 'And I especially want to thank someone who made us all shine like stars. The ab–so–lute–ly a–maz–ing, Mister Sax!'

A cheer goes up that transforms into a chant, and then Jamal's calling him up.

'Mis–ter Sax! Mis–ter Sax!'

I hand him the microphone.

'Thanks, Leonard.'

Mr Sax holds his hands up and gets a hush.

'Thespians, people, I'm humbled. You don't know it yet, you're too young, but these memories you've made, these friendships you've forged, will be some of the sweetest things you will have in your life, some of the purest, most sublime moments you will experience. It's a wild world out there.'

Cheering breaks out and it pumps Mr Sax; he gets even more lyrical.

'Yes, out in that big wild world, you may be seared by the heat of the sun, you may despair at the winter's rages. But what will give you shelter and strength, will be the friendships made working with these magnificent pages!' He brandishes the script. There's applause and shouting because they love his word-poetry.

'Rhyme!'

'More!'

'Yes, we performed the show only one day. Was it worth it? Of course. I was the Artistic Director. Yet it wasn't only me who made it happen. So many contributed. The cleaners who made sure when you lay on the floor doing exercises you weren't covered in muck – some of those cleaners are your mums, so thank them. The costume-maker, Carla. Mrs Podborsky who did all the music, what a marvellous job she did, yes? The set-builders, their fabulous painted designs, including the marvellous if shaky balcony scaffolding. The lighting team. The sound production team. The make-up crew. The dressers. The dance instructors. The voice coaches. The social-media stars who made sure we had an audience. Endless. The poster designers.

'But most of all, yourselves, here. Who stuck with it. Through tears. Through disappointment. Voices breaking. Hearts breaking. Injured toes. Outbreaks of fisticuffs. You had the audacity to dream. You've been magnificent. And if you can remember this courage, this togetherness, and take that with you out into the wild world, you'll make that world a wondrous, wondrous place!'

'Speech!'

'Oscar for that man!'

Jamal hits a party tune but Mr Sax starts waving to him and Jamal fades it down so he can speak again.

'Nothing grand now. Just remember your homework extensions are from this day invalid because the play is over. Get your homework in on time, don't end up in Mr Chips' soul-destroying detention class. OK, enough. Enjoy yourselves!'

Jamal works the sliders and it all kicks off. Horse is busting moves again in his wedding-style shirt and his red winkle-picker shoes. Eddie's in there matching him and Ronay's doing rub-a-dub with Adele. The gymnast girls are throwing shapes. The party's too hot to handle.

I look around. Some of the set is still standing. I realize I'll miss Tia's leg trembles before she goes on stage. I'll miss Malik's card-tricks on breaks. I'll miss Stefan's snorting laughter. The way Liam always sweeps his hand through his hair before he says any of his lines. I'll miss the group hugs and the daft exercises. How Andrea always seems to trail perfume wherever she goes. They'll all disappear back to their classes and I'll never see them except maybe a glance while running along a corridor. I dance all these thoughts away.

There's a commotion at the doors. Sheba's grandma bursts in. We make room and she gets into the middle of us and starts hand dancing. We join in – it's like a slow motion fruit-picking mime. Sheba's mum spots her and leads her back off. Sheba sneaks in while her mum's back is turned. Her head is going left and right.

'Looking for me?' I ask her. I've come up behind her.

'Maybe,' she says.

We stand together. The tempo slides up to the scratchy graveyard beat.

'Let's zombie!' she yells.

'Look to the left, avalanche!' I call out. It's the cue from the play for the biggest dance.

Everyone immediately drops into zombie mode. We lock step – all of us. Even Mr Sax and Mrs Podborsky. We're like one breathing person in that moment, totally together, synching weight-shifts, hip shimmies, foot-spins. We're doing the lowered-into-the-grave move when Sheba's sister finds her. She hauls her off, apologizing to us all by tapping her wrist. Time.

Sheba shrugs a goodbye as her fingers slip from mine. All I can think is: Why not let us have this one night of fun? Then Eddie's jumped on my back for the flesh-eating-meltdown move. We're flat on the floor giving it the electric shocks when Carla appears above me, tapping her wrist. What is it with adults and wrist tapping?

The Punto's fully loaded. Carla stops off at a warehouse where she's renting a container for the costumes. The entrance is surrounded by barbed wire and CCTV camera poles. I help Carla haul the first lot of costumes into the foyer. At the reception desk, there's an old guy with washed-out green eyes who looks like he needs a week of continuous sleep. He buzzes the gate to the containers corridor open. We step through.

He calls out: 'Where's he going?' He's pointing at me.

'With me,' Carla says. We've both got our arms full of costumes.

The reception guy puts down his vending-machine coffee and shakes his head. 'Only customers go through. There's been a run of thefts and we're having to do everything by the book. He has to wait here. I'll make him a coffee if you want.'

Carla looks like she's about to kick off but I drop the costumes I'm carrying and tell her, 'Go ahead, it's OK.'

She disappears down the corridor. I go out to the car to get more costumes. As I come back in, I see this spiky-haired man and spiky-haired boy get waved right through. Carla's coming back up the corridor and sees it too.

'What about them then?' she says.

'They're regulars,' the reception guy says. 'They're known.'

'That's by the book then?'

'It's my book. If you don't like it, go somewhere else.' He goes back to playing on his phone.

We drive off. We take a few traffic lights in silence before the moment at the storage centre is forgotten. Carla asks me about the kiss. Her voice is in pure nosy mode.

'It was just a kiss,' I tell her. 'It was in the script.'

'You didn't look like you were complaining,' she says.

'Why didn't Mustapha come?' I ask, changing the subject.

'We only had two tickets and he wanted our mum and me to be there. He'll come next time.'

The idea of a next time makes me smile.

We're stuck at traffic lights again. Carla starts singing my falsetto song. I know she's teasing me but I can tell that actually, she loves the song. After a while I join in. That's how we arrive home at one shade after midnight – wailing that song.

PART 3

PEAK ZOMBIE

Carla swings the door open and Mum immediately puts me in a hug that is probably also a legitimate jiu-jitsu move. I'm just about to lose consciousness when she releases me. She says she's cooked me beef-burgers and chips as a treat and to build up my strength after all that singing and dancing.

'Quick warning,' says Carla over all the commotion. 'He's at Peak Zombie. He's been doing zombie dancing all evening. He's seen the zombie footballers mid-show, according to his Drama teacher. And he's naturally high as a kite right now, after all the cheers and applause. You have been warned.'

My sister kisses me.

'Oh, by the way, lickle brother, I need to take some photos of you in the costumes.'

'No. No way,' I say, starting into the beef-burger as I talk. I've already eaten two. Mustapha's just slipped his on to my plate so this is my third.

'Oh, go on. It's to promote my company.'

'No.'

'After all I've done for you and your mates? All those costumes I made – up all those hours sticking needles in myself?'

'No way.'

Mum intervenes. 'You two stop arguing. Carla, I'm sure he'll have a good think about it. Ask him tomorrow. Leonard, I know you are a "thespian of the highest quality".'

Mum's quoting Mr Sax and loving it. She continues: 'But even brilliant thespians need their beauty sleep.'

'Has Mustapha got his own toothbrush yet?'

'Ask him. He's sitting next to you.'

'I hold my hands up,' he says. 'I'll go get one from the corner shop.'

'Yeh, do that,' I tell him.

'Leonard. Manners,' Mum says. Then, to Mustapha: 'He's tired.'

'Anything else, Lenny?'

'No,' I tell my mum. 'I love you, Mum.'

'You still have to go to bed.'

'But it's M.M.A. Fight Night.'

'No.'

She's decided.

Mum exits to the kitchen, Mustapha exits the front door to go to the 24-hour corner shop and Oklahoma enters, stage left, jumps on the sofa, snuggles herself into my lap and starts purring. I look at the living room, trying to see it through Oklahoma's eyes.

Mum: the feeder but also the chaser with a broom.

Carla: the provider of nice long strips of cloth to claw at.

Mustapha: on the floor, one of Mustapha's golf balls with the strange clacking noise its dimples make when you roll it around the living-room floor until the chaser starts chasing you.

There's the beginnings of the stair carpet. Okla likes to steal up to it, then suddenly throw herself on her back and attack it with all four paws. Oklahoma has three sleeping places. The window-ledge. My lap. And right in front of the television. Mustapha chucks rolled up socks at her if she gets between him and his TV programmes. That makes him Mustapha the sock chucker.

Oklahoma casts an eye up at me as if in confirmation, then goes back to studying the walls. Maybe she can hear mice in them. We had mice once. That's probably why we've now got so many cats.

Mustapha comes back in and plonks himself down next to me, scaring Oklahoma who flees to her place in front of the television. He waves a newly bought toothbrush at me, takes off a shoe then starts rolling up one of his socks.

Mum comes in with a big hammer and a handful of nails, which scares both me and Carla.

'What's that for?' asks Carla. She's back behind her sewing machine and about to start her *zzz zzz zzz-ing*.

'I'm nailing his window shut.' She turns to me. 'Over my dead body are you ducking out of that window to visit zombies tonight.'

Mustapha stops her. 'Nah, you can't do that.'

'Why not? I'm not chasing him across fields at silly a.m. I've got that job interview.'

'It's fire regulations, isn't it? That's his best exit in a fire.'

Mum sits down, flummoxed. 'What then?'

Later, in bed I hear this tinkling sound at my door. I get up and find my mum and Mustapha rigging these chains of little Christmas bells to my bedroom door.

'What the ****?' I ask them.

'So we'll hear you if you open the door. There's more going on your window.'

I try to block Mum off but she sails past me. She tacks a chain of Christmas bells to my window-frame with a flurry of hammering that scares away all the cats. 'Don't you dare take them off,' she says, turning with the hammer still in her hand.

This is what I have to put up with.

I lie back and find the football book. I've not picked it up in ages. The football team were out in force at the After-Party and there's no way me and Sheba can duck out of re-joining. They've had terrible results but the Cup competition starts soon. It's the middle of winter now. The pitches will be mud.

There's this photo of a match taking place in the middle of a gale. The football book starts glowing. I feel this tingling. Everything in the photo goes vivid. The rain's chasing around the stands. The players have pulled down the sleeves of their shirts so they cover their hands but I can see the goose-bumps on their legs. The window rattles. I hear the bells shimmer. It's the equivalent in sound to the shimmering spotlight on the stage.

I let the book drop as memories of the show float back into my mind. I recall things I never knew I'd noticed. Like how someone chucked a paper aeroplane on stage during the kiss scene. Like I forgot my spoken lines after the kiss and went straight into the dance. The plot was wacky: lots of running round in the countryside, a dance-off, then Juliet is paralysed with Rohypnol and Romeo thinks she's dead. He's about to kill himself when the Rohypnol wears off and

Juliet wakes up. Then comes the duet. Followed by the kiss.

It's strange. The play lasted ninety minutes. Yet in those ninety minutes, I lived what felt like a lifetime. And in that fraction of a moment when we kissed, it felt like forever. Yes, it was a stage kiss. Yes, it was two actors, acting professionally, on a stage performing for an audience. But it was also me and Sheba. And her lips were on my lips. And that is as real as it ever gets. Sheba kissed me and I kissed her and it was one hundred times more than beautiful. I can still feel her lips on mine when I close my eyes. I'm there again and she's kissing me.

There are the two things I decide I love. Acting and football. The Windmill was right. I have too big a passion for football to ever let it go. I live it, eat it, breathe it, and hear it. Would I let it go for another kiss?

I can hear something now, although it's very faint. A referee's whistle. The zombies are out on the park again. I get out of bed, pull on my clothes and ease open the door.

I hurry through the fog till I find them. They're running up and down, fog swirling in their wake. I watch their training exercises and memorize them. Knee-high jumps. Sideways bends. Toe-touching. Zig zag running. Then they start practising long passes. The ball zooms out of the low-lying fog into the air then zooms back into the fog again – yet they can always see it because the ball glows orange. They let me join in. I do shooting, tackling and piggy-in-the-middle exercises.

There's a shout: 'Leonard!'

Someone on the sideline. A shadow. A familiar one. Mustapha. He's wearing a woolly hat and his Superman dressing gown. He's in slippers. I break off from the practice and run over.

He has a resigned look on his face. 'Don't tell me. Playing football with the zombies again?'

'Can't you see them?' I ask him. 'They're all here. Bobby Moore. Jack Charlton. Geoff Hurst. Nobby Stiles. Ray Wilson. Jimmy Greaves. That's who I train with most, Jimmy Greaves, because he was like me, he didn't get a game, especially in the Cup Final. He didn't get to play.'

'What are you rambling on about?'

'He's waving to us. Jimmy Greaves. You can't see him?'

'There's nothing and no one there. Only fog. Lots of swirling, freezing fog.'

A ball flies loose. I trap it under my boot. 'What's this then?'

Mustapha sighs. 'Nothing there, lad.'

'There is!'

'OK, OK. So what are you doing with them?'

'Training. They're passing on tips.'

'I don't see them. I wish I could. Maybe it's because they're not heroes to me.'

'Like they won the World Cup and they're not heroes?'

'There was this black player John Barnes. And Jimmy Greaves, after he'd retired from football and everything, he was doing commentary. And he knocked Barnes bad, saying he didn't try hard for England because he was black. Greaves could never be a hero to me after that. And if all the 1966 team was like him, then like I say, they're not my heroes.'

'Well, they're my dad's heroes and that makes them mine!'

'Whatever.'

'And by the way.'

'What now?'

'You know you said my dad was in prison because Mum said he works on an oil rig?'

'Forget it.'

'You're wrong. He really does work on an oil rig.'

'My bad. Go and play. Go ahead.'

'One last thing.'

'What?'

'How did you know I was here?'

'I heard the bells.'

I drift back into the fog and they let me play in their six-a-side. It's a great game, full of sliding tackles and booming shots. I score twice and I get handshakes from all of them before Geoff Hurst blows the final whistle. I hear the whistle warbling but I hear the tinkle of bells too. The Christmas bells Mum put up round my window. *Maybe I've dreamt all this?*

Everyone wants to know you when you're famous. The morning after the musical, I'm mobbed at the school gates and even though I'm dog-tired, I do selfies with people left, right and centre. My phone's burning with Likes, Follows, Alerts and Thumbs-Ups. People bust zombie moves wherever I walk. Some sing my songs back to me. It's great. I start practising my signature and wondering if maybe I need an agent in case Hollywood calls.

Of course, it doesn't last. By lunchtime everyone's forgotten. Except the football team. A deal's a deal. They expect me at training.

All day I look for Sheba. I text her a couple of times but get no reply.

We've got double sports in the afternoon because a teacher is off ill. The Windmill's ready with news of who we're playing in the first round of the Cup competition. I call the team together and tell them that if I come back it has to be my way. Nobody argues. The Windmill doesn't mind: 'We've tried everything else,' he admits, 'so we might as well try Lenny's stuff, however crazy his ideas. Welcome back, Lenny, we've missed your miserable face!'

With his help, I lay out a training circuit for the team. High jumps. Star jumps. Two Touch triangles. Then long-range passing. Everyone joins in, even Eddie who grumbles about the amount of running involved from point to point. By the end of it, The Windmill says he likes the plan. 'It's a back-to-basics approach, Leonard. Keeping it simple. Pass and move. Hoof it high. Very Japanese Method. I'll draw it up on the flipcharts.'

I give The Windmill a thumbs-up because I know he enjoys drawing up charts.

My phone goes off in the changing room. It's a text from Sheba, finally. It begins with *Hi Janice* so I nearly delete it thinking she's got the wrong person, but I read it anyway. She's got flu. Her mum has banned her from Drama Club – which is fine because the show's over anyway. I text her back and she says she's still able to do football matches but no evening training and her sister has to go with her everywhere. Also, she's not allowed to zombie dance in the house because her grandma dislocated her shoulder doing the zombie roll after she came home from the show.

She ends the text with: *Bye Janice* CTF POS 😊 😷 😂 🤪 😌

The letters stand for 'Warning: Can't Talk Freely: Parent Over Shoulder'.

Mum's in tears when I get home.

'What's the matter?'

'I got it.'

'What – the flu?'

'No, the job. I am a real, proper chef, Leonard!'

She jumps up and we dance in a hug. I hear sniffles at my shoulder. Mum's still crying.

'So what's up?'

'I can't take it.'

'Why not?'

'It's nights.'

'So?'

'I'd be worried sick about you and your zombie sleepwalking.'

She's sitting down now. Mustapha has come clumping downstairs. He puts an arm around Mum. 'Here's an idea,' he says.

'What?' Mum mutters.

'I take him training in the early evening. Maybe the zombies can put in a shift then instead of leaving it so late. What do you say, Leonard?'

I shrug. I've never heard them play early evening. 'I'll give it a go,' I say. 'You know what really works though?'

'What?' They both say it at the same time, turning their heads to me at the exact same moment too. It looks funny.

'Lenny?' Mum asks. 'Spit it out!'

'The cats. When the cats are in my room, they stop me somehow.'

'Sorry?' says Mum, confused.

'Why don't we try both?' says Mustapha. 'You do your trial at the restaurant, Julie, I'll sort out Leonard with early training. And we'll let him have the cats in his room when he goes to bed. Deal?'

He holds a hand out, flat. Mum puts her hand over his and looks at me. I put my hand over hers. 'Deal,' I say.

Carla bursts in right that second. She sheds a whole heap of bags on to the floor, a bunch of perfume samples which she scatters on the glass coffee table, a bag of broken biscuits that she plonks into the fruit bowl, and a set of brochures for a photo studio that she spills on the sofa.

'What's this then?' she asks, looking at us with our hands together. 'Thieves' convention?'

'Zombie pact,' Mustapha replies. 'But tell us your news, darling.'

Before Carla can speak, Mum bursts out, 'Carla, I got the job! Well, a six-week trial first but ...'

'You got the job! You got the job!' Carla squeezes the life out of Mum, then does a dance that scatters the cats.

'All those mushroom risottos and koftes paid off?' Carla says in wonder, when she finally calms.

'I guess so,' says Mum, suddenly shy.

'And we're sorting his zombies out,' Mustapha chips in. 'Gonna let him train earlier in the park, see if that does it.'

180

'Not too early though,' Carla says. 'I've booked a studio at five p.m. tonight. He's got to model costumes for my brochure.'

'When did I agree to do that?' I protest.

'Lickle brother, you owe me big time. You're doing it.'

So that's how I find myself in a little flat in Ancoats taking instructions from a photographer who's making me feel like I'm a Paris-Based Top Model:

'Turn to the left. Now to the right. Can you pout? How about a moody sulk? Good. Hold that … and again. Keep that. Good boy. First-class, darlink, you've got the look. Hold it. Can you tug the tights up a little, they're slipping? Good. And the doublet at the waist, yank it across. Excellent. The camera loves you. You're a natural, a star.'

Bing!

Flash!

Someone dabs powder stuff on my forehead. A big reflector shield is at my feet. I pose as if kicking a ball. Then as if I'm falling backwards. Then looking up as if calling Juliet, but higher, on the toes more. 'Hold that for five seconds. And sulk. Good. More weight on the front leg. Stretch! Further, further. Raise one eyebrow. The other one. A bit lower. Lift your chin a centimetre higher … and *hold.*'

It's tough, modelling, and I'm exhausted by the time the hour's up. Carla bundles me back in the car with the costumes and drives us home. I notice Mum's car seems to have become Carla's.

Mum's cooked my favourite ham and onion omelette – for energy. I gulp that down then Mustapha whizzes me to the park.

181

'Go on then,' he says. 'Get training with your "friends".'

'They're not here,' I say. I look around at the empty park. I'm as disappointed as he is.

'Train anyway,' he says. We've brought a ball. 'I'll help out.'

Me and Mustapha do a thirty-minute session, mainly long passing. Darkness drops fast and by the end I can hardly see the ball.

I'm about to call it a day when I hear a clacking sound. I look about. The boy with the wooden rattle is standing at the side of the field. He shouts. 'Go on, smash it in the net!' Not at me. At somewhere beyond me.

I turn around again and peer into the murk. This time I can just make out, further down in the park, the faint, smudge shapes of the zombie team.

'They're here,' I whisper to Mustapha. 'They're here!'

'Keep the faith, yeh? If you want to join them, go ahead.'

The boy with the rattle calls out: 'Run like the wind, Leonard, get yer foot in there. Tackle 'em!'

I run to join the zombies.

Mum's left the house by the time we get back. Mustapha checks my window bells, makes sure all the cats are in my room, then gives me the thumb-up. I pick up my *Philosophy Book*. I find some good stuff in it. *Fame is fickle. Success is never certain. Every day brings something unexpected. Being is becoming.* I haven't a clue what that last phrase means so I fling the book to the floor and pick up my football book.

I read two pages on England's 1966 tactics and what the England manager, Alf Ramsey, decided was the best way to play each game. Then I look at a photo. It's a bright day. A full stadium. A player on the centre line is leaping for the ball. As I look, the page comes alight. It glows brighter and brighter. I hear the faint shrill blast of a referee's whistle. A match is being played somewhere.

I sit up in my bed.

All three cats line up on my bed, staring right back at me.

MUD, MIST AND GLORY

Sheba has recovered from flu and she shows up at break-time next day. I'm leaning on the building behind B Block with Eddie, seeing how far we can spit. Sheba's wrapped in a long, new blue coat that has a thin collar in the style of TV detectives. She comes and stands where Eddie was standing. I've not heard from her for so long I'm annoyed.

We blow fog clouds for a few moments. Then I ask her, 'Why didn't you reply?' I mean to my texts.

'Why – did you miss me?'

'I was worried about you.'

I glance at her. She turns round so she's facing me and stands a little closer. She's close enough I can feel her breathing through her coat.

'My phone's being monitored now,' she sighs. 'They've even put Location Tracker on it so they can know where I am at any time and where I've been.'

'They've banned you from drama?'

'Yeh. And I'm not allowed to hang out with you.'

'Why?'

She looks at me like it's a stupid question. Then she shrugs. 'I'm not allowed a whole list of things.'

She holds two fingers out wide to show how long the list is.

'Like what?'

'I'm not allowed to go football training.'

She stubs her toe on mine then her foot slips over mine and stays there.

'And?'

'I'm not allowed to stand close to you.'

I nod. 'Carry on.'

'To gaze into your eyes.'

'Like this?' We're so close I can feel the heat of her face on mine.

'It's a long list,' I murmur.

'Umm. It goes on for ever.'

She's so close now I can smell her lip balm.

'Yeh. I'm not allowed to kiss you.'

'You sure?'

Eddie's back. 'Are you two canoodling?' he asks, bursting between us.

'What's that?' asks Sheba.

'She's not allowed to football practice sessions,' I say. 'Her fam have banned her.'

'Shit,' says Eddie. And he spits a long one.

'If you want to learn the throw-in, I can show you now,' Sheba says.

'And we can film any training sessions you miss,' I suggest. 'Then put them on YouTube and you can join in.'

'Let's do it,' says Eddie. He puts his arms round both of us and we run to the pitch. The throw-in line's been churned up by the rain and it's only just visible. Sheba takes my ball.

'Right. Technically it's a front flip throw-in,' she says as me and Eddie wait for her demo.

'That's me out then,' says Eddie. 'I can't do a front flip.'

'I can,' I say. 'Eddie, you go out there and try to head it when it comes over.'

Eddie jogs on down the pitch.

'OK, here it comes,' shouts Sheba to Eddie. She takes the ball and does a five-step run up, then her head and arms go down in a charge to the grass. Her hands, with the ball clenched tight in them, hit the ground and she rotates her whole body. As she comes up, the ball whips up and into the air. It goes so far past Eddie he has no chance of heading it.

'Got it?' she says to me, grinning. 'It's like a flying, rotating, hand-stand.'

I have a go. I get the run-up right but my arms crumple when my hands hit the ground and instead of whipping forward I end up in a mess of limbs in the mud. Out in the field, Eddie's killing himself laughing at me. Sheba hauls me up.

'It helps if you've done gymnastics. You need core body strength and good abs. Have another go.'

I try again and again and I nearly make it work one time.

Sheba stands to the side and when I'm in mid-front flip turn next time, she puts a hand to my lower back and helps me rotate. The ball flies like an arrow out of my hands and way beyond Eddie. He watches it fly past him and keep on and on.

'Wow,' says Eddie.

Even Sheba's impressed. 'It's all in how you use your back right here,' she says, placing her hand on my lower back where it already feels sore.

'Is that allowed?' I say.

She does this curl of her upper lip that's a little bit of a smile, but mostly annoyance.

Eddie jogs up. 'What about me though?' he says. 'Can't you teach me something?'

'OK,' says Sheba, 'here's another one, without the flip.'

The same day, after school, the team gather for an unofficial practice. We planned to train on the school pitch but it's waterlogged. We take off to the nearby park but that's under water as well. The only place we can think of is the cemetery overflow - the stretch of grass that's waiting for new graves to be dug. We go there.

I show everyone how to do a front flip throw. Only three players in the team manage it – me, Marcus and the goalie. Eddie shows them the second-best technique, using your back but not doing the flip. By the end, we're all getting much more distance on the ball. The goalie is the best.

I then teach them the latest stuff I picked up off the zombies. Half volleys. Kick and rush. Side foot tackling. Penalties.

'Where d'you learn all this stuff?' Marcus quizzes me.

'Books and YouTube,' I lie. Only Sheba knows about the zombies.

Darkness creeps in. I can still see headstones of real graves in the used part of the cemetery, but only just. Someone mis-kicks the ball. Its black and white checks spin through the air in a graceful arc. It lands far from us, among the used graves. Everyone looks at everyone else. No one wants to go and get it.

187

'Who's going?' I ask.

Seven fingers instantly point at me.

'Fine.'

I trudge through the wet grass. Something darts beneath my feet. *A mouse, only a mouse.* I keep walking. The grass makes this slushy sound that joins the sound of tree branches groaning in the wind. There's a tap on my shoulder. I spin round. *The branch of a tree.* As I walk deeper into the cemetery, the mist thickens until I've lost my bearings. There are graves everywhere. I stumble over one and can't help putting my hands out to steady myself. The gravestone reads:

In This Wet Earth Lies … Taken Before Her Time.

The name of the person has been rubbed out by wind and rain and moss. Wet stuff from the leaves on the trees drips down my arms and slides along my back. I shudder. *I can't see the ball anywhere, I'll have to go even further in.* I sweep my legs through more long grass, trying desperately not to tread on the old graves. *Why did no one come with me? They're supposed to be my friends.*

My phone goes off. But stops ringing as suddenly as it began. I pull it out of my pocket to check it. It's out of charge. In the half light, far away through the mist, I can see the shadows of Eddie, Marcus and the rest. Normally they'd be fooling around by now, but they're waiting quietly for me. I look and look and look for the ball but there's too much dark, there's too much mist.

A gruff voice startles me: 'Must be somewhere.'

I look up. It's the zombies. They're scattered around the graves and are searching, like me. One of them calls to the others, 'Right here! By the feet of …' He leans over and reads the gravestone. 'Arnold Stockton. Nifty player in his time.'

He picks the ball up and throws it to me. It wallops my stomach. I run back with it. I've never been so thankful to see Eddie's glistening face.

'You shot out of there like you'd seen a ghost,' says Eddie. 'How'd you find it so quick?'

I laugh. 'I've got X-ray eyes, Eddie, X-ray eyes!'

When I get back, Mum's not in and Mustapha is groaning on the sofa. 'I'm too tired to train tonight,' he tells me. 'There was a staff shortage at the depot and I've had to do two extra rounds. My legs are killing me.'

'That's all right,' I tell him. 'I already went.'

It startles him. 'Where?' he asks, sitting up.

'The cemetery.'

'You went football training in the cemetery?' Mustapha flicks both his hairless eyebrows up and sighs.

Later, he wedges me in my room with the three cats and hands me a pair of ear plugs. 'Might stop you hearing the whistles or whatever,' he says.

I take them, but as soon as he leaves my room I pluck them out of my ears and chuck them on the floor.

I listen to Jamal's football commentary podcast. The one where we lose 13:0. That was then, I think. This is now. We're a different team now. I wonder when Jamal's going to load the next one. He's a great commentator. It's a pity he broke his eye-socket and can't play football any more. Life's like that sometimes. Bad stuff happens. I don't need my *Philosophy Book* to tell me that.

I remember how I used to fight with Marcus and then he went deaf. For weeks, I blamed myself, thinking maybe

189

somehow I caused it by stressing him. He plays better than ever now, Marcus. Maybe I should invite him to train with me and the zombie team. Nah, he'd think I was nuts talking about training with zombies.

I listen out for the zombies, but all I hear is the cats, purring.

An amazing thing happens next Saturday. We win a football match. I'm so stunned my mind goes blank and I can't remember any of it except I scored a goal. My mum's text wings its way into my phone as I'm getting dressed.

Never mind, darling, it's only a match, keep on trying xxxMumxxx

I can't wait to get home and tell her, if only I can remember what. I wave a quick goodbye to Sheba. Her sister's been all over her since the end of the match and is steering her to her car. I race home, not bothering with the bus because it's too slow on Saturdays. Mum's yellow car is outside the house so she's not left for work or anything. I look in every room but I can't find her.

'Mum? Mum! Mum!'

She comes chasing down the stairs with the house phone in her hand and looks like she's been arguing about bills.

'What's up?' she says.

'Nothing. We won, Mum, we won!'

Mum screams and drops the phone. Then we're jumping together.

'And I scored. It was 2 nil. We're in the semi final!'

Mum sobs. 'I always knew you had it in you. You worked so hard at it. It used to break my heart – ask

Carla – to see you so unhappy. I'm so proud of you.' She looks down at the floorboards. 'Are you there?' she shouts angrily at the floor. 'You should be proud too!'

'Who are you talking to?' I ask.

'Your dad. He's on the phone.'

I pick it up. The line's dead. I press Redial. It rings out with no answer.

'Liar!' I tell her. Why does she have to spoil things by making stuff up?

'He really was,' Mum shouts up from downstairs as I slam the door on my room. I hear her voice faintly, though I know she's still yelling. 'It's a bad line, he's in the middle of the ocean, for crying out loud!'

I don't believe her. Sometimes Mum treats me like a kid, telling me things I want to hear instead of telling me the truth. I pull my headphones on and play music loud enough to cancel everything out. I'm on Track 3 of Dizzee's new album when I see this piece of paper slide under my door.

It's a brochure, advertising Carla's costumes. The front panel has me in the doublet and green tights, leaning forward like I'm being dangled over a river, and scowling like somebody just stole my pocket money. The humiliation. I wonder why I bother getting out of bed.

I pull out my *Philosophy Book* and flick through to the Index at the back. Under *Misery*, there's a three-page subsection on something called Stoicism. Stoicism is commonly understood to mean knowing that things are awful and putting up with them – but it actually means avoiding all extremes of emotion. I throw the book on the floor. The Stoics should try living my life.

Mustapha pushes all three cats into my room.

191

'Get out!' I tell him.

I find the football book and look up the 1966 players' childhoods. I realize Geoff Hurst grew up near me. That means, every day I'm walking the same streets Geoff Hurst used to walk. Bouncing my ball off the same walls. Running in the same patches of grass. I look across at the window. It's pitch black outside now. *I can hear the clacking of the boy's rattle.* I turn a page. The book begins to glow. I feel this tingle. Faintly, I catch the *peep peep* of the referee's whistle. I go to get up.

The cats surround me.

I lie back down, let go of the book and tune my phone to Jamal's podcast of our Cup game. The one we've just won. I go to sleep listening to it.

Jamal's Podcast

The Blue Devils are standing tall in their new blue kit. They're coming onto the pitch old-school style. Knees up, running. Next will it be a short back and sides haircut? Who knows? It's the Blue Devils. The band of brothers plus one girl.

And she can throw a ball. She's doing a front flip catapult throw, head over heels. The first ever in the tournament. The ball soars like a javelin. Eddie's rocketed up and his head makes contact, crashes it into the net. Gooooal! Space Station, we have lift-off! Devil may care how he managed to jump so high. Or how she managed to throw like that.

The opposition are scratching their heads. It's 1 to the nothing for the Blue Devils. I repeat in case you thought you misheard. It's 1 to the nothing to the Blue Devils. This match is legend already. Ain't no stopping us now.

Here goes Marcus on a mazy run. He passes it. That is not a broadcast error, people. Marcus actually passes the ball to another player. Kwong hoofs it up the pitch. It's got to land on somebody's head. No … everyone misses it. It bounces high. Now, Leonard comes in. Leonard with a low diving header. The net balloons. It's 2! Slap me with a wet fish! Two to the nothing. Let the trumpets sound. Let my dead grandmother shake her batty. It's a score-sheet to go down in history.

I'm speechless. This is Jamal Podcast on 873.5 also on Twitter and Insta and everywhere else. I'm speechless. Jamal's Podcast. Blue Devils Run Amok. That's the headline. Two to the nothing. That's the bottom line. The Windmill's flapping with joy. This is Jamal, speechless. I need a cold drink and a dark room. I'm on Twitter and everything else. Jamal, speechless. Beam me up. Two to the nothing. Fade me down. Two to the nothing. Jamal. Speechless.

It's semi-final day. We're in the changing rooms, ready to hit the pitch. I've spent all week running the practise sessions. Will it pay off? The Windmill bustles into the room in his white Nike tracksuit. His grey eyes flick around the room. Marcus. Nod. Horse. Nod. He catches my eye and nods. I fill up with tears and pride. I have to look away. *Breathe.*

'Right, boys.'

The Windmill slides his fingers through his hair, tugs at his ginger beard, looks down at his clipboard, up again, down again, clears his throat. 'Everybody decent? OK, come in, Sarbjit.'

It's a routine now. Sheba comes and sits next to Eddie, which is three places from me. Her sister hovers by the changing-room steel doors.

'OK, team for today is Leonard, Marcus, Horse, Kwong, Sarbjit, Eddie, Nat ...'

My name was called first. I sit back and let feel-good vibes fill me up. The tears well up again. *I've got to get this under control.* I glance at Sheba. She ducks her head and shuffles my way. We knock fists behind Eddie's back.

The Windmill starts some flip-chart stuff – sliding different coloured magnetic pieces around as he describes how he expects the opposing team to play and what we should do to counter them.

'We'll play a high line today, OK?' he says, moving three green pieces on the chart. 'And I want lots of pressure on the ball.' He moves four red pieces into a group. 'Forward line, give it lots of width and movement. Midfield, keep one defensive guard working as a sweeper linking with defence, everything slick two-touch.' Six more pieces, both green and red, fly around his chart. 'That's it. Marcus, take all the free kicks, Sheba, take all the throw-ins and aim them for Eddie – high balls in for him. Kwong, be ready for the knock-downs. Leonard, you're on penalties. Any questions?'

The plastic pieces have been zipping up and down the flip chart with dizzying speed. Most of them have ended up around the opposition goal, so I figure The Windmill wants us to put their goalmouth under siege.

'Excuse me, sir,' asks Kwong, 'but what's a high line?'

'Keeping the ball in their half. Playing the game in their half. Clear?'

194

'Yeh,' says Kwong unconvincingly.

'Anything else?'

'Are the showers working?'

'Andrew! This is a semi final you're about to play, and you're thinking how hot are the showers? You fly up that wing and get the crosses in, don't worry about whether you can shampoo your hair after. Play your hearts out. That's it.'

There's a pause. It's like something's missing but nobody knows what. I put my hand up. The Windmill sighs.

'Don't tell me, Leonard. Look, lads, I'm not Mr Sax, I don't know how to do big speeches. But imagine I've made one right now. Go out and play as if I've made a big, fighting speech. Got it? Good enough, Lenny?'

Everyone laughs. The Windmill closes his flip chart. 'Right, off you go.'

There's a new edge to us. I look around and see what I've never seen ever before. It's not confidence. It's expectation. We expect to win.

Jamal's outside with a microphone and does a quick interview with Horse. I do a high-five with Sheba. This is only the second time we're playing together in midfield.

The game kicks off and the opposition come at us with a series of sliding tackles. It's fierce and nasty, but we fight. Horse upends some of their players and gets a free kick given against him that they score from. But, unlike in the past, our heads don't drop. Andrew does a cross that Marcus gets his head on and Eddie wins the goalmouth scramble and scores. Then Marcus is fouled in the penalty area. I pick up the ball and place it on the penalty spot. I see this flickering zombie in front of me. Jimmy Greaves. *Keep a cool head.*

I remember what I worked on with the zombies when training one night – how to fool a goalkeeper when taking penalties: *Look left, shoot right.*

I stroll up. *Look left, shoot right.* The ball smacks into the back of their net with their goalie stranded. People are slapping my back. Bear-hugging me. Trying to pick me up. I hear a wooden rattle whirring like a hawk. The boy from the photo is there on the sidelines, jumping for joy. More faintly, I see the zombies around him in suits and ties, watching too. Jimmy's among them. They put their hands in the air, then get their combs out and tidy their hair up again.

'Lenny, concentrate!'

It's The Windmill, shouting at me.

The referee spots the ball for a kick-off but then immediately blows a long trill to end the game. 2:1. *We're in the Final.* I feel dizzy.

Over on the touchline Jamal's jumping for joy with his microphone. Sheba runs into her sister's arms. There's no one's arms on the touchline for me to run into, but me, Marcus and Horse fall into a muddy tangle on the pitch, celebrating. We've reached the Final. Who would have believed?

I get up out of the pile only for Andrew to jump on my back. Then Kwong grabs my cheeks and twists them, yelling in my face, 'We did it! We're in the Final! Believe!'

In front of us, The Windmill heads back to the changing room. He walks the same way as those people crossing the hypnotist's waiting room. Floating. And The Windmill was right. No one minds when the showers don't work. We leave the school ground caked in mud and glory.

That night I play and replay Jamal's podcast.

Jamal's Podcast

Leonard to take the kick. He places it on that shiny splodge of white known as the penalty spot. He moves his bandy legs eight equal steps backwards. Rome wasn't built in a day. The weight of an empire rests on his shoulders. I wouldn't like to be in his shoes right now. He's stubbing the grass with his worn-out old Pumas. His trusty old boots. He bends down. What's he doing? He's picked up a piece of grass, holds it to the sky. Now he drops it. He's seeing which way the wind blows and how strong.

The goalkeeper in front of him is as big as a Goliath and is jumping up and down like an Angry Bird. It's the Angry Bird versus the Blue Devil. Leonard pauses. The referee signals with his hand for him to take the kick. Leonard's talking to himself, I can see his lips moving. What's he saying? A prayer? It will be *Glory Glory Glory* if this hits the back of the net. I can't imagine how he'll feel if he misses but probably like being hit by a bus and I've felt that. Painful.

Leonard's on his run up. He leans back. Left foot down. Right foot swinging through. *Boom! Bakooshah!* Goal! Holy moley! Slap me with a wet fish! Drown me in the MISSISSIPPI! It's raining happiness! It's raining glory! It's raining! And I'm getting wet! Leonard. Cool as a frozen cucumber. Calm as a dozing Yoga teacher. Precise as a Casio 85EX Calculator. Leonard the Lion! He took that penalty perfect.

This is Jamal, Speechless on Podcast 835.6. On Twitter, Insta. On everything else. It's 2 to the 1. The referee gives it a long, rasping blast on his whistle. That means one thing. It's over! We've won! Blue Devils in the Final. Remind me who I am! Remind me what day it is! Run me over.

197

Raid the fridge! Rewind. Rewind. I'm speechless. This is Jamal, Speechless. Fade me down. Speechless …

I get back home.

'Mum? Mum!'

'Hi, love.'

My mum's in the kitchen. She's got a gleaming new set of knives lined up on the worktop and she's picking them up and putting them down like a Ninja preparing for battle.

'Well?'

'What?'

'How did it go?'

I'm trying to play it cool but I can't any more.

'Aaaagh! We wooon!' I jump up on the stepladder Mum uses to reach the top kitchen cupboards and shout it again in case she didn't get it. 'We won. We're in the Final!'

The ladder wobbles to the left. Then to the right. Then collapses. Mum catches me just in time and hauls me down. She sniffs my hair. 'I'm so proud of you.'

'Thanks, Mum.'

'Have a look in there,' she says, excited.

I follow her into the living room. There's a parcel sitting on the table. I pick it up. It has my name on it.

'I've had a few more phone conversations with your dad, and …'

'Mum!'

'It's the truth. He's sent you that parcel. It's yours. It's all sealed and that. Check the address. Unless I've flown off on a sudden holiday in the Seychelles, I haven't sent it.'

I pick the thing up. The sender's address ends with 'The Seychelles'. I shake it. Just a few clumpy sounds. I tear off the plastic wrapper, burst through the inner brown paper and rip out the box within that. A shoe box. I flip open the lid. Football boots. A brand new pair of red Nikes. My size. From my dad. I hold them at the heels and turn them round and round. Exactly the ones I wanted.

'Don't cry, Lenny, love, you should be happy. You wanted them, didn't you?'

I nod.

'Try them on then, good lad.'

Mum leaves for work. I feed the cats. They're not interested in my football story but they have to listen anyway – that's the price of the cat food I'm spooning out for them, I tell them. Carla bursts in.

'Who are you talking to?'

'The cats.'

'Oh Lordy.'

'We won.'

'Pardon?'

'We're in the Final.'

Carla does this short, high-decibel scream. Then she smooths her hair, straightens her top and calmly says, 'That's amazing. Here's a fiver.' I love my sister.

'And Dad's sent me these boots.'

'Don't be silly.'

I point them out. She holds them up, frowning.

'Look …' I show her the packaging. I've folded it on the table, sender's address up.

Carla studies the label a long time. I know it's not Mum's handwriting.

'Not a birthday card in ten years,' she finally says, 'but this makes up for everything.' She's being sarcastic.

I shrug.

'Was there a note with it?'

I shake my head.

'Nothing for me?'

'I didn't see anything.'

Carla runs upstairs and locks her bedroom door.

This house should have revolving doors. Ten minutes after Carla's dashed out to her boyfriend's, saying she won't be back tonight and to tell Mum, Mustapha staggers in and collapses on the sofa. He says his workload keeps going up and his back's killing him. He lies there groaning so convincingly I get up and make him a cup of coffee, the first time in my life I've ever made him one. He sends it back twice for more sugar. Finally, he notices the boots on the table.

'Nice,' he says. 'Yours?' Like there's a possibility Mum or Carla might have taken up soccer as a hobby.

'Yes,' I say, then add, as nonchalantly as I can, 'from my dad.'

'Soak them in warm water,' he says, just like that.

'Why?'

'Break them in. You can't wear new boots straight out of the box.'

It's like he hasn't heard they're from my dad.

'Course you can,' I tell him and laugh at his idea.

'Fair enough,' he says. He goes back to groaning, and in between groans, sipping.

I watch him. He's looking at me. I'm looking at him. I'm waiting for him to ask. He hasn't got a clue so I mime heading the ball a bit.

'Oh right, yeh. How did the match go?' he asks.

'We won! We're in the Final!'

He shoots up and bear-hugs me. 'Brilliant, I knew you could.' He releases me. 'You played all ninety minutes then?'

'Yup!'

'Fantastic.' He falls back into the sofa. 'You must be tired. Maybe skip the training tonight, yeh? You don't want to overdo it.'

'Sure.' It's Mustapha who wants to skip training, not me, but I'm fine with that.

'Listen, take a hot bath to stretch your muscles else you'll get cramp in the middle of the night. Then get your head down early tonight, yeah? I'll get the cats up to you. Try to go straight to sleep. OK, champ?'

I know what's on his mind. 'I've seen the zombies already today,' I tell him. 'They only ever call once a day.'

'Just in case then.'

'Fine. Whatever.'

'And well done, our kid. You're in the Final.'

'I even scored.'

He adds smiling to his groaning and sipping faces. I can tell he's really happy for me, even though he's not given me any money.

I take the bath. It feels good. Then I slide into bed. The cats are already there, waiting at the end of the bed, watching each move I make. I try to lean over and pick up one of my books but it's as if someone keeps moving the floor further and further away from my hand. I fall asleep before my hand ever finds the bedroom floor.

DON'T LOOK IN THE MIRROR

It's the day of the Final. Mum says Dad's flying in from the Seychelles to watch. I arrive at school in a hurry for lessons to end so I can get on the pitch, but time doesn't cooperate. According to our science teacher, one second lasts exactly the same amount of time as another. Today, every second decides to dawdle and drag, retrace its steps, hang around. Every minute turns into enough time to fill a hundred grandfather clocks. I decide not to look at any devices with time on them because they're all in a big conspiracy to annoy me.

I say my name at each class register call-out yet I still pick up three Detention slips and I don't even know what for, but I don't care. I'll stay a month in Detention class next week if that's what they want, I just want to hear the home-time bell. The only time that the seconds speed up is when Jamal decides to mess about in Citizenship Studies and gets sent out for it. It went off like a tennis match:

'Socrates was a very skilful arguer. Jamal, are you paying attention?'

'I am now, miss.'

'Why are you at school, Jamal?'

'Because my mum would beat my backside if I didn't go, miss.'

'You are at school to learn. In order to learn you have to listen.'

'But I can learn from books, miss, that's not listening.'

'You will learn nothing from arguing.'

'But you said Socrates was a skilful arguer. So arguing is a skill you can learn, miss. By practising, miss.'

'Go and stand outside, Jamal.'

'Which part of outside, miss? It's a big place, outside.'

'Now.'

'That's impossible, miss. Because when you said "now", that moment is already gone. You could say "get out within five seconds". Unless, miss, when you say now, you mean a floaty now – a springy, spongy, floaty now.'

'Floaty now.'

Jamal moves his rangy limbs as floaty as the first moon-landing man, all the way from the back of the class to the classroom door, and disappears outside.

The teacher's looking for a fight now. 'Anyone else?' she says.

It's the last lesson. Time has slowed to a halt. In desperation, I get my phone out, plug in an earphone, run the wires and earpiece up the inside of my sleeve and out by my hand then hold my hand to my ear and listen to Jamal's podcast of the *other* semi final – the one that decided who we'd be playing in the Final.

Jamal's Podcast

This is Jamal, at the other semi final, keeping it quiet in case they rumble me. The mighty Aimtrue Academy is on this earth but not of this earth. Rumour is they eat only raw fish and new-born babies. They're rampant.

The other team's a quivering wreck. Aimtrue lead 9:0. The other team is being slaughtered. Aimtrue have run through the other team as fast as a butcher with his bits on fire. They're pinging the ball around like the mad flippers of a berserk arcade game.

... The whistle blows. Aimtrue have just won 14 to the nothing. Aimtrue are a machine. They've crushed everything in their path. Jamal, speechless, fading down. I need to get moving now so I get out alive. Jamal, Podcasting on 873.5. Aimtrue. A relentless killing machine. And the machine's coming our way. Blue Devils best watch out. Jamal, speechless ...

I tuck the earpiece into my sleeve because the teacher has started walking round the class. I get busy pretending to write. She eyeballs me, takes a step towards me but then someone calls out and she goes back to help them instead.

I'm drowning in time again. The teacher starts explaining something to do with the movement of water molecules and my brain turns to treacle. I check my phone clock. It's not shifted since I last checked. Lessons are like software updates. You're sure they're 99 per cent finished, but when you check, you're still at 5 per cent. The body of the teacher starts flickering. I imagine her becoming a pile of bone dust in a school building that crumbles to brick dust, then trees shoot up and I'm sitting in a zombie wilderness. I feel this tingling.

Finally, the home-time bell rings. I'm first out of the door and run over to B Block.

Yelling, dashing, whooping, the team assembles outside the changing rooms. Horse goes around shouting, 'We can win!' Jamal's interviewing everyone about if they have any rituals or superstitions, whether they slept well last night, if they had any dreams about what the score would be. Balls are flying through the air and bouncing off windows. The Windmill arrives and opens up. We scramble inside.

I add a final dab of polish to my new red boots. My dad's coming to see me play. I can't believe it. My heart beats like mad and my eyes well with tears. I've kept the boots fresh for this match because I want my dad to see them at their best as I fly past, spreading panic in the other team. The film of the match will be called *Boots on Fire* and I'll play myself as the hat-trick hero.

The Windmill calls the team out. My name is called first again. Sheba and Eddie are in too. There's five substitutes because, after we started winning, all the players who left have come running back.

Sheba nudges me. She's wearing a new head-wrap, grey this time instead of the usual black. The light in her eyes is a mixture of excitement and fear. I've told her about how my boots are from my dad and he's flying in to see me. I nudge my toes to test how well the boots fit. They're snug. She watches me take the boots off then pull them on again and lets me lean on her to do the laces up. I realize that, of everyone in the room, Sheba is the one I want sitting next to me right now.

Me, Sheba and Eddie are lined up together on a bench again. But this time we're about to play in a Cup Final. Sometimes life's amazing. Eddie grunts something into his mouth and swallows it. His face is beaded with sweat. They've fixed the boiler but the radiators are jammed and the heat's risen to sauna levels. Eddie starts beating out a tune on the floor tiles with his football boot studs. I recognize it. So does Sheba. More boots join in. Sheba throws her head back and bursts into the song from our Musical duet:

'We will win! We will shine, we will overcome!'

On cue, I splice my line in:

'We will find a way, our best race to run!'

Soon the whole changing room is ringing with the song and the drumming of boots. It's the sound of hope and defiance and guts.

The Windmill waves his blue clipboard in the air:

'All right, lovely to hear that, now let's get down to tactics! Gather round.' He turns the cover page of his flip chart. There are eight colours to the tabs now and the tactics sheets go six pages deep. We follow along as best we can as he whirls through it all. The end chart has us in four rows so I think he wants Eddie to play on his own up front, Kwong behind Eddie, four midfielders and four in defence. He's got these sticky coloured strings running around the last chart as well and at least sixteen black arrows pointing in every direction. Me and Sheba swap a puzzled look but hide it.

The Windmill wraps up: 'They'll probably come at us fast at the start, OK? So be strong, keep your positions. All right?'

There's nods and murmurs. We're as ready as we will ever be. The Windmill says he's not happy with the energy he's getting from us. He gives it another try.

'Who do we fear?'

'Nobody!'

'Louder. Who do we fear?'

'Nobody!'

'That'll do.'

We trot out. I look around. My dad's nowhere. My mum's there though and explains that my dad's flight got diverted due to strong winds, but he might yet make it – I mustn't despair.

The first half is a disaster. Everything Jamal said could happen came true. They slice through us. We can never get hold of the ball. Meanwhile, the new boots are killing my toes. I'm in tears. I keep going but I'm hobbling and it's useless. Again and again, Aimtrue run through our midfield like it's not even there. I can't chase back. Their passing zings round us. Horse gets angry and starts fouling. Marcus starts trying to dribble through their entire team, which makes things even worse. We never win any throw-ins for Sheba to take.

I look along the touchline. I can see my mum. I can see Sabbi's sister. But there's nobody there who could be my dad. I remember my dream from last night. It was the Final – and as I ran up the wing I noticed somebody standing next to Mum who had this close resemblance to Carla. Same nose. Same eyes. Same cheeks. His hair was flicked out in a big Afro and he was wearing ankle-length boots and a brown fur coat. A cluster of diamond rings sparkled on his fingers. He grabbed my arm as I ran past.

'It's me, your dad!' he said.

I stopped running, shook his hand and laughed. 'Dad, I'm in the middle of a match!'

'Boots any good?'

'Thanks, great. I've scored two in them already and I fancy a hat-trick.'

My dad's cheeks puffed with pride in the dream. 'Get that hat-trick. Do me proud, son.'

And I did. In the dream.

The Windmill's screaming at me from the touchline.

'Leonard, wake up! Defend! Defend!'

There's a cheer behind me. I turn. Aimtrue Academy have scored again. Their fourth.

The referee blows half-time. 4:0. There's gales of laughter from the Aimtrue team as they walk to their touchline. They're shaking their heads at how bad we are, pointing and jeering at us. It's like they're already celebrating their victory.

I trudge off the pitch. Mum puts an arm around me. 'Never mind,' she says. 'You did your best.'

'Shut up, Mum, it's only half-time. Save it for when the match is over.' I have this flashback of all those texts she used to send me. Saying it right in my face is even worse.

The Windmill comes up. 'He's not running properly,' he says to my mum.

Mum shrugs. I've got my hands on my knees, in deep pain from the boots. The Windmill bends down so he's at eye-level with me.

'I'm sorry, Lenny, but I'm going to have to haul you off ...'

'Wait! Wait!' It's Mustapha, running up. 'Mr Houghton, he's wearing new boots.'

'I noticed.'

'Lenny, get these on.' Mustapha pulls something out of a shopping bag. My old boots. The ones I'd thrown out with the rubbish. 'Don't sub him yet, Mr Houghton. He pulls these old ones on and we'll have the old Leonard back. I guarantee.'

The Windmill scowls. 'You only get one chance at a Final.'

'Five minutes,' says Mustapha. 'That's all. See if it works.'

'Tsk.' The Windmill isn't liking the idea. Behind him, the subs are bouncing up and down trying to attract his attention.

'Please,' begs Mustapha.

Sheba and Eddie have come over and are right by my side now.

'Go on,' says Eddie.

'A million times please,' begs Sheba.

'I feel good now,' I say to The Windmill, meaning with my old boots on again.

The Windmill sucks his teeth, glances behind him, then back at me. Finally, he says, 'I'm too soft but OK, five minutes.'

Mustapha winks at me. I nod a *thanks* back to him. Sheba does a crazy dance with Eddie.

'Right lads, gather round,' calls The Windmill. Everyone drifts closer. 'Four zero is not so bad,' he says. 'Keep going. It could be worse.'

Horse blows a flail of snot out of his nose.

Someone steps forward. It's Mr Sax. He's arrived with Carla. 'May I say a few words?' he asks The Windmill.

'Be my guest,' our coach says.

'Hold hands,' Mr Sax commands us. 'Everyone.'

We're confused, but we do it.

'Come close. Closer. Closer … good.' Standing at Marcus's shoulder, Mr Sax drops his voice. 'They're confident over there, aren't they? Look at them. Swaggering, joking, thinking they've got the Cup in the bag. But you've only played Act One – there's plenty of time to turn this round. Agreed?'

There's a muted 'Yes!' from all of us.

'We can come back,' adds Horse. 'Now Leonard's got the right boots on.'

'Damn right you can come back. You're the mighty Blue Devils. Walk like Blue Devils, run like Blue Devils. You can do that?'

'Yes.'

'I didn't hear you.'

'Yes!'

Mr Sax calls out. 'Carla, get your blue paint!'

Carla comes running over. 'Pardon?'

'You still have the greasepaint, don't you, in your car? Get it and make them into Blue Devils again. That's an order. Go to it.'

Carla runs off. We're still in a huddle.

'Has anybody seen the New Zealand rugby team perform their Haka?' he asks.

Nobody has. Mr Sax drops into a Kung Fu-like stance and we move back to watch.

'They strike fear into the opposition,' Mr Sax says. 'We'll not do the Haka but we can do a blood-curdling yell. Something like this.'

He lets out a yell that shakes the trees: 'Aaaaaa … *ha!*'

The parents are coming closer, intrigued. The Windmill has edged forward. Mr Sax motions to him and he stands next to Mr Sax then drops into the same stance. Mr Sax and The Windmill bump fists.

'It's like summoning the energy of the universe,' continues Mr Sax, 'putting fire in your belly. It means this is your time, this is your moment. Now let's all do it – our Blue Devils yell. On the count of three, with me.'

We squat in a low stance. Then on Mr Sax's 'Three!' we slap our thighs and do the yell.

'Aaaaaa … *ha!*'

The sound bounces around the field. It gets the other team's attention. It gets everyone's attention.

'Now rise up, Devils,' says Mr Sax, 'and make this second half your comeback time!'

Carla's swift with the paint. She smears all our faces. The Windmill has abandoned his tactics talk and is going around getting everyone to practise the 'tongue-out' yell. I look around. Suddenly, with our faces daubed, we look fearsome.

The whistle for the restart goes. As I walk on to the pitch, I feel this tingling taking over my entire body. And I see that shadows are walking on with us. It's the zombies, in their old kit. It looks like we've summoned them too. I nudge Sheba. 'Can you see?'

She nods, stunned. This time she's seeing them.

I look up. All our team's gazing. For the first time ever, they can see all the zombies and they're pointing at them.

The Aimtrue team can't see anything except us, pointing. They look scared.

When the match restarts, we've got shadows who run alongside us, showing us when to move, when to pass. Jimmy Greaves runs with me. My feet fly. I hear the boy in the crowd's wooden rattle flailing in the air as I storm towards the goal, Jimmy Greaves at my shoulder. I dink the ball round three players and smash it into the net.

Jimmy turns, hands held high. The '66 team run up and high-five him. I've got Sheba on my back, Horse riffling my hair, Marcus saluting me.

Aimtrue Academy can't handle our new slickness. We claw the game back to 4:4.

'One more time!' Horse drives us on. It's the eighty-ninth minute. I slot the ball through to Marcus. Marcus spreads the ball wide to Kwong who dashes up the wing with it. He gets tackled and it's a throw-in. The Windmill's screaming for Sheba to take it. Kwong stuffs the ball in her hands. Sheba takes a long, bouncy run up then launches herself at the touchline, flips head over heels, releases the ball and it flashes through the air. Eddie's up. Jimmy Greaves has left my side and is running in there. He leaps too. Eddie's airborne and twisting his head to the ball. Jimmy Greaves stretches his neck out at the same time. They both head it. The ball sails easily over the Aimtrue keeper and into the net. 5:4.

Eddie's running, arms aloft to Sheba. Jimmy Greaves is running up to the zombies in the same way. The boy with the rattle has run on to the pitch to celebrate. He thinks it's all over. The referee checks his watch and blows his whistle. It is now! Jimmy Greaves spins and cartwheels. Eddie's disappeared on a lap of honour round the pitch. I fall to my knees in tears. We did it. We, the no-hopers, we won the Cup. I'm in a daze all the way to the changing room.

Above the clatter of boots thrown off, a song goes up. 'We Are the Champions!' We sing it at full, lung-busting volume.

'Hurry up, the showers are broken again. Get dressed, get dressed!' shouts The Windmill. 'You've got a teammate wanting to join you!'

The singing doesn't stop as we clamber into our clothes. Then Sabbi's at the door with her sister, who has her in an arm-crushing hug. Sabbi breaks away. Her sister goes to grab her but Sabbi's too fast. Then me and Sabbi are arm in arm again and she's hugging me to death as everyone joins in the singing.

'Champions ... of the World!'

Somewhere amid the madness I see The Windmill roll up his flip chart and chuck it in a bin. He looks the happiest I've ever seen him. The celebrations get even livelier. Cans are sprayed over heads. I run along the line as the team sings my name, high-fiving every player to the end of the line. I see the '66 zombies flickering on the far wall, like a fading cinema projection. I run to the back of the dressing room to reach them. At first they go to shake hands with me, then, joining in the spirit, they high-five me instead. Jimmy's last.

'Thanks, mate,' he says, tears in his eyes.

'We're cool,' I say.

The team's calling my name louder. I jump on a bench and join in the singing. I glance back at the wall. They've gone. The '66 side have faded away. It's just us now. Jamal's in the front row of the party, throwing rock-star shapes. He's made up this chant that everyone's shouting:

'We've got blue in our hair –
Do we care? Do we care?'

Sabbi's sister comes up to me. 'Thanks,' she says.

'What for?'

'For making my sister happy.'

'That's OK.'

213

'She talks about you a lot.'

Sabbi's at her sister's shoulder and gets embarrassed. She pushes past her sister and strangle-hugs me to stop me saying anything. Everyone cheers. The singing starts again. Then half the team's on their phones to text and tweet the news. Parents come in. The Windmill's handing them leaflets about a fundraiser to get the pitch drained. Sheba's sister looms over us.

'Come on, Sarbjit, time to go.'

Sheba squeezes my hand. Her sister ushers her away.

The celebrations continue so long I don't remember when I leave the changing room or how I get home.

Next morning, Mum explains there was a squall and Dad's plane had to turn back but he's sent me another parcel. Carla says he's become a chequebook dad because she just found out he's put money in her account so she can go to Milan Fashion Week. Mum overhears her and does a wincing smile.

I wait for my parcel. It takes five days. When it finally arrives, it is not boxy like the last one. It's heavy. I rip off the brown wrapping paper. It's a football book:

Brazil: World Cup Winners 1970: The Beautiful Game in Full Colour.

Mum tries to rip it out of my hands. 'You're reading that over my dead body. We're not chasing round parks in the middle of the night any more!'

I cling on to it though. Mustapha laughs at us and says, 'Let him have it!'

That night, I open the book up. The players are wearing shirts as bright as the sun. I feel this tingling. The book

214

begins to glow. The distant sound of samba drums comes to my ears. The cats start hissing.

I put the book down because I'm thirsty and tiptoe to the bathroom. I switch the light on. Something makes me look up at the mirror.

There,

        staring right back at me,

                is a zombie.

DON'T MISS
THE OTHER BOOKS
IN THE STRIKER SERIES

'Full to the brim with the joy, heartache and passion for the beautiful game.'

Carnegie Medal winner, Melvin Burgess

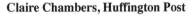

'Mehmood gives us a sterotype-quashing, timely novel about religion, gender, and families. You're Not Proper sounds a resonant, authentic note that cuts through the monotone voices coming out of YA writing'

Claire Chambers, Huffington Post

'An innovative, impressive and well crafted narrative that strikes a chord for young and old alike'

Carol Leeming

Lightning Source UK Ltd.
Milton Keynes UK
UKOW05f2130110717
305131UK00002B/461/P